P9-CFB-685

TRAINING YOUR
GERMAN SHEPHERD DOG

Brandy Eggeman and
Joan Hustace Walker

About the Authors

Brandy Eggeman is a certified dog trainer and behaviorist with more than 30 years' experience training German Shepherd Dogs and various breeds. Additionally, she has worked as a Search and Rescue canine handler for the state of Virginia for more than 17 years and is a tester and evaluator for the American Kennel Club Canine Good Citizen Obedience program, Therapy Pets Unlimited, and The Foundation for Service Dog Support, Inc. She also works with the Virginia German Shepherd Rescue in the rehabilitation of dogs with behavioral issues so that they can be adopted out as quality, lifelong family members.

Joan Hustace Walker is the author of more than 20 pet books. She has written hundreds of feature articles, has photographed hundreds of published images, and has received more than 50 national and international awards for her vast body of work.

A Note on Pronouns

Many dog lovers feel that the pronoun "it" is not appropriate when referring to a beloved pet. For this reason, German Shepherd Dogs are referred to as "he" throughout this book, unless the topic specifically relates to female dogs. No gender bias is intended by this writing style.

Cover Credits

Shutterstock
> front cover and back cover: Grigorita Ko
> inside front cover: Mikkel Bigandt
> inside back cover: otsphoto

© Copyright 2018 by Barron's Educational Series, Inc.

All rights reserved.
No part of this publication may be reproduced or distributed in any form or by any means without the written permission of the copyright owner.

All inquiries should be addressed to:
Barron's Educational Series, Inc.
250 Wireless Boulevard
Hauppauge, New York 11788
www.barronseduc.com

ISBN: 978-1-4380-1050-2

Library of Congress Catalog Card No.: 2017952210

Printed in China
9 8 7 6 5 4 3 2 1

Acknowledgments

I would like to express my gratitude to the many people who saw me through this book; to all those who provided support, offered comments, and assisted in editing, proofreading, and design. And, to all who have helped me and worked with me over the years, thank you.

I would like to thank Joan H. Walker for the friendship and laughs, as well as all the help she provided in making this book happen. Thanks to my editor, Angela Tartaro. You made this an enjoyable experience.

Above all, I want to thank my husband, Mark Eggeman; my son, Austin; and my daughter, Brianna. You guys are invaluable with all the help you provide. My family supported and encouraged me in spite of all the time it took me away from them. It is truly a family affair. Thank you to all the dogs that have taught me so much. This would not be possible without them. My many German Shepherds, both past and present, have each taught me something new: Bayja, 13 years; Ekko, 10 years; Biene, 5 years; and my knucklehead Rock, 4 years. And, last but not least, to the Australian Shepherd, who "thinks" she is a German Shepherd, Stormy, 5 years. My heart dog Bayja … I will never have another like you.

—Brandy Eggeman

Photo Credits

Shutterstock—Albert Russ: 77; Albin Hillert: 125; Andrey_Kuzmin: 22; Anna Aibetova: 5; Bandak Dmytro: 81; cat3n: 4; cherezoff: 90; DanyL: 61; Dora Zett: 42; elis_aksenova: 10, 12; Eric Isselee: 31, 48, 99, 144; Ermolaev Alexander: 41; everydoghasastory: 30; Faraonvideo: 88; Fesus Robert: 58; Grigorita Ko: vi, 2, 6, 19, 20, 23, 34, 37 (top), 46, 51, 68, 104, 114, 126, 145, 164; Happy monkey: 37 (bottom); Hugo Felix: 25; Hysteria: 63; Ivan Azimov 007: 113; Jagodka: 92; Julia Siomuha: 66; Julien_N: 80; Kachalkina Veronika: 153; KELENY: 70; Ksenia Raykova: 154; Kurashova: 76; Lenkadan: 139; Luca Nichetti: 91; marcin jucha: 87, 107 (top), 107 (bottom); Melory: 3; Mikkel Bigandt: 163; Mirko Graul: 29; Monika Wisniewska: 83; Natalia Fedosova: 108; Nicky Rhodes: 101 (bottom), 123; NSC Photography: 161; OlgaOvcharenko: 84; rokopix: 71; Rolf Klebsattel: 157, 158; Rosa Jay: 28; Rosalba Matta Machado: 55; SikorskiFotografie: 59; Sonsedska Yuliia: 21, 117; Stone36: 57; Tiplyashina Evgeniya: 94; Vivienstock: 112; VP Photo Studio: 121
iStock—bas0r: 155; Carmelka: 131; fotokate: 8, 18; HDKam: 74; cunfek: 142; NNehring: 13; pawprincestudios: 73; Radekk: 14; SashaFoxWalters: 16; Sharon_Mendonca: 38, 70; Tom Kelley Archive: 15; Wavetop: 129
Fotolia—Nicky Rhodes: 100
Woof Tracks Photography—26, 45, 50, 52 (top and bottom), 53 (top and bottom), 64, 67 (top and bottom), 86, 89, 93, 96, 98, 101 (top), 103 (top and bottom), 106, 111, 115, 116, 119, 120, 122, 123, 135, 137, 138, 147, 149, 150, 151, 156

Contents

1. **The Well-Trained German Shepherd Dog**   1
   Life with an Untrained German Shepherd Dog   1
   Benefits of a Well-Trained German Shepherd Dog   3

2. **What Makes the GSD Tick?**   7
   History of the German Shepherd Dog   7
   Characteristics and Drives   17
   How Challenging Will This Training Journey Be?   24

3. **German Shepherd Dog Training 101**   27
   Approach to Training   27
   Learning Capabilities of the Puppy, Adolescent, and Adult   27
   Home Schooling: Working with the Rescued
       German Shepherd Dog   32

4. **Housetraining**   35
   Your Pup's Urges and Abilities   35
   "Gotta Go" Cues   37
   Making the Crate Comfortable   38
   Does My Crated GSD Need to Relieve Himself?   39
   Creating a Routine   41
   Special Tips for the Rescued German Shepherd Dog   44

5. **The Well-Socialized German Shepherd Dog**   47
   Genetics Versus Environment   47
   The Importance of Understanding Body Language   48
   Behavior Pathways and Physical Expressions: Green-, Yellow-,
       and Red-Light Behaviors   49
   Socialization with People   56
   Socialization with Dogs   62
   Socializing the Rescued German Shepherd Dog   65

6. Habituation 69
Handling Home Introductions with the GSD Puppy 69
Give Your GSD a Safe Observation Place 70
Training *Place* 70
Preventing Separation Anxiety (SA) 72
Treating Separation Anxiety 73
Training *I'll Be Back* 74
Thunderstorms 76
Noise Aversion 77
Light Chasing 78
Car Travel 78
Home Habituation for Rescued Adult Dogs 82

7. Beginning Command Training 85
Training Tools 85
Ways of Learning a New Behavior 86
Reinforcements: What They Are and How They Work 88
A Question of Timing 89
Benefits of a Great Trainer and Training School 91
Home Schooling: Clicker Training Basics 93

8. Commands Your German Shepherd Dog Needs To Know 95
Here or *Watch Me* 95
Collar Touch 97
Sit 99
Stay 100
Down 102
Come 104
Heel 106

9. Additional Helpful Commands 109
Off and *Up* 109
Stand 111
Take It and *Out* 112
Leave It 113

10. Preventing Problem Behaviors 115
The Importance of Exercise and Mental Stimulation 115
Mouthing 116
Barking/Whining 117
Teaching *Quiet* 118

Bolting   118
Teaching *Wait*   119
Teaching *Get Back*   120
Counter Surfing   120
Destructive Chewing   122
Digging   122
Fence Jumping   123
Jumping Up   124
Self-Mutilation   125

11. Aggression   **127**
Owner-Directed or Dominance Aggression   128
Fear Aggression   129
Territorial/Protective Aggression   129
Three Types of Dog-on-Dog Aggression   130
Chase/Predatory Aggression   133
Possessive Aggression   134
Aggression Toward Babies or Children   135
Redirected Aggression, Frustration-Elicited Aggression, and
    Barrier Aggression   136
Food-Related Aggression   137
Play Aggression   138
Social Aggression   139
Medically Based Aggressions   140
Sex-Related Aggression   141
Hyperactive Aggression   141
Reactive Aggression   141

12. Activities for Your German Shepherd Dog   **143**
Non-Competitive Events and Programs   143
Non-Competitive Service Activities   146
Fun, Outdoor Activities   148
Competitive Activities   151
Home Schooling: How to Register for Events Without Papers   162

Useful Addresses and Literature   **165**

Index   **168**

Chapter One

The Well-Trained German Shepherd Dog

The German Shepherd Dog has long been a favorite among pet owners, as well as those involved in working, service, and performance events. In 1926, the German Shepherd Dog was ranked No. 1 in the United States and has maintained a "top ten" presence for decades. In recent years, the German Shepherd Dog has held the No. 2 spot for nearly two decades.

The breed's popularity is understandable. The German Shepherd Dog is widely recognized as being highly trainable, intelligent, courageous, and loyal. Intelligence comes with its own set of disadvantages, however. German Shepherd Dogs are not just smart, they are super smart, which means they are not the breed of choice for those who are inexperienced with dogs and/or who are inexperienced training dogs.

If there is any breed that needs training and the establishment of leadership, it is unequivocally the German Shepherd Dog. In other words, the German Shepherd Dog will not train himself. If left *untrained*, he will do his best to *train you*.

Life with an Untrained German Shepherd Dog

So, what would life be like if you didn't take the time and effort to train your German Shepherd Dog? The following is a glimpse of what you're in for.

As a puppy, your GSD will be wonderful. He will follow you around like the hopelessly adorable little guy that he is. He's cute. He's fluffy. And, his intelligence will be obvious from the get-go. But, he will be content being a puppy and letting you introduce him to his new world.

Then, adolescence happens somewhere around six to seven months. Hormones begin to kick in, and that sweet little puppy is now a nearly full-grown dog—and he is beginning to show behaviors that you may not be enamored with. He is not as eager to follow you around. He starts to test his boundaries. And he is large enough in size that his attempts to push you around may become intimidating.

When he was a puppy, you could just lift him off the couch and there would be cooing and petting and puppy kisses. Now, you can't lift him, and if he doesn't want to get off the couch, he's not moving. Herding behaviors that were so cute when he was tiny aren't so cute when he is bigger and actually herding children into corners of your home. The little gnawing on your fingers has now turned into harder mouthing. Walks used to be enjoyable, but now you are being dragged down the street by a very strong young dog and, if he hasn't been properly socialized, you could have a barking mess on the other end of your leash.

But, the troubles don't stop there! Poor manners in the house and on walks create challenging moments that can quickly escalate. Friends and family members can't come over because your German Shepherd Dog will knock them down and argue over seating on the couch. Putting him in a crate in the garage or a far room temporarily solves the problem, but it doesn't improve the unwanted behaviors. Excessive crating of a high-energy and high-drive dog causes a whole host of new issues, as the dog is not being exercised and is isolated from his human family. Training seems like a good idea; however, beginning a program now can be a daunting task, and sending the dog to a trainer can be costly. So, the adult German Shepherd Dog may be relegated to the backyard, where he scratches at the screen door because he wants to be inside, digs mammoth pits in the ground because he's bored and/or stressed, and perhaps he even starts escaping over (or under) your six-foot fence.

Your beautiful, sweet, intelligent puppy with so much potential has become a 65- to 95-pound (29- to 43-kg), active, full-size German Shepherd Dog that you have absolutely no control over. Tragically, at this point, many people feel helpless and may end up relinquishing the dog to a shelter. Or, if he's very lucky, he is brought to a shelter or a rescue organization that has the resources to carefully evaluate him, work with him, and slowly bring him back to his true potential so that he can then be placed successfully in a new home.

If this sounds like it couldn't possibly happen, sadly, it happens every day to German Shepherd Dogs across the country. The vast majority of GSDs that wind up in rescue usually do so through no fault of their own; the dogs' poor behaviors are nearly always a result of lack of socialization, lack of training, "training gone bad" (i.e., dominant, aggressive, or abusive training), lack of exercise, and/or lack of mental stimulation.

When a German Shepherd Dog does not have any rules, when he's not required to respond to certain commands, when he's allowed to think that no one in his human family is in control, it is not a matter of *if* he will take over, it's more a matter of *when* and *how*. The GSD needs structure and leadership to succeed—both of which can be accomplished through positive training.

Benefits of a Well-Trained German Shepherd Dog

Now that you're aware of what can happen if you don't train your GSD, what can you expect if you put the time and effort into training?

You're in control. Worried parents, skeptical neighbors, and fearful dog owners will appreciate that your large working dog is well-mannered, sociable, and completely safe to be around. It is plain to see that he is obedient and listens to you. The trained, calm, and social German Shepherd Dog is a good ambassador for a breed that can be feared by some and labeled by others as "dangerous."

He's walkable. This is a big one. If your German Shepherd Dog is dragging you everywhere, even if he's not barking at people or other dogs, you aren't likely to take him anywhere. If he's walkable, however, you will be more likely to take him everywhere he can legally go! Good leash manners take time and effort to train, but it is well worth it for both your dog's health and your sanity.

Your German Shepherd Dog accepts you in a leadership role. A daily training routine not only helps to satisfy your dog's

need for mental stimulation, but it puts you in a leadership role. The big plus of this is that leadership is established through daily, positive reinforcement and *not* physical punishment.

Training helps establish gentle leadership for children, too. Once you've taught your German Shepherd Dog to respond appropriately to commands and make sure he is solid on them, it is important to involve your children (if you have any) in working with the dog, too. Children aged 10 and older (and some mature 8- and 9-year-olds) are capable of learning how to train dogs, and some can even train at a competitive level! Children who are younger (4 to 7 years old) can learn to give the GSD commands *with* you next to them or right behind them to make sure the GSD responds cor-

rectly to your little one's commands. Many dog trainers and dog training schools encourage families to come to classes so that everyone learns how to train the puppy. Children younger than 4 years old can learn good pet owner manners (see page 59) and can be raised to be kind and gentle with the puppy as he grows into an adult dog.

He is fun to live with. Anyone can come into your home without worrying about being jumped up on, knocked over, barked or growled at, etc. There's no need to crate this dog when you have people over. Children are welcome, too. Basically, your visitors' only worries may be how much dog hair attaches to their dark clothing but hey, they *know* you have a German Shepherd Dog.

Travel is a snap. If you have a crate, harness, or SUV barrier, then you're ready to travel with your German Shepherd Dog. When your GSD obeys your commands, can settle in "place" (see "Training *Place*," pages 70–71), is easy to walk with on trails, knows to leave other (wild) animals alone on your "leave it" command (see "*Leave It*," page 113), car travel will be easy. And, whatever your destination is—a park, campsite, hiking trail— your German Shepherd Dog knows how to behave when he gets there and, of course, he listens to you and obeys your commands.

The bond you share will be deeper. Though German Shepherd Dogs make great family dogs, they tend to bond more deeply with one person—usually the one who spends the most time with them. If you are training your GSD, you will be that person. If you haven't experienced the depth of a bond that can form through training, you are in for a wonderful surprise.

Potential problems are more easily recognizable. Prevention is the best cure for behavioral problems, but early intervention is the next best thing. If a problem is present, it is much easier to correct or modify the behavior if it is recognized early as opposed to trying to correct or modify a problem that has existed (and has been reinforced) for months or even years.

Your German Shepherd Dog can live in more places if he is trained. The good news is that if you train for the American Kennel Club's Canine Good Citizen (CGC) test and receive a passing score, (see "CGC," pages 143–144), your GSD's CGC title will open doors for you. As you might know, the German Shepherd Dog is on many insurance companies' blacklists as a high-bite risk. As such, not only do GSD-owning homeowners find they can't get homeowners insurance, but potential GSD-owning renters may be denied housing in otherwise dog-friendly apartments or rental homes. German Shepherd Dog owners also may not be able to move into military housing, as the breed is on the banned list of some bases. That's the bad news. The good news is that having the CGC title on your GSD often will qualify you for a waiver—not only to live in rentals and military housing (that have a ban on certain breeds), but also to have a homeowner's insurance policy with insurance agencies that have the GSD on their blacklist. A dog, regardless of the breed, with a CGC title is recognized more and more as being a good citizen and a lower risk for biting or harming someone in the home.

As you can see, the benefits of training your German Shepherd Dog far outweigh the risks of letting him grow up on his own. In fact, in order for him to become a treasured companion, he *must* be trained. He will be happy learning from you, and he will be happiest when he has a true leader to work for.

Of course, the fact that you are holding this book and reading this chapter indicates that you know this. Training is the key. And, along the way, you'll probably discover how much fun it can be to train your dog, ultimately creating a bond that few people truly experience.

Chapter Two
What Makes the GSD Tick?

To understand the drives and characteristics that make the German Shepherd Dog both enjoyable and challenging to raise and train, it is important to appreciate what went into making this breed.

History of the German Shepherd Dog

As with all of today's purebreds, the basis of what is now the German Shepherd Dog originated from someone's desire to create a dog that was better at performing specific tasks than any other dog. For the GSD, that task set was performed previously by up to three different "specialist" dogs: herding dogs that kept large flocks together on unfenced lands; farm dogs that worked with livestock, sorting, penning, and driving animals to market; and livestock guardian dogs whose only job was to ferociously drive away wolves, bears, and human poachers.

Prick Ear Shape

Wild dogs around the world, as well as the wolf, all have what is called "prick" ears, or—naturally erect ears. The GSD, along with the sled-pulling breeds, (e.g., Siberian Huskies, Alaskan Malamutes, Samoyeds, etc.), some Terriers, and northern "spitz-type" breeds (e.g., Akita, Shiba Inu, etc.) are examples of domesticated dogs that have naturally erect ears.

Multiple types of herding, farm, and livestock guardian dogs were used in developing the German Shepherd Dog. Early GSDs were white, sable, tan and black, solid black, and brindle. Coat types varied from shorthaired and longhaired to wirehaired, as well as single coats and double coats. Ears ranged from erect to folded and tail carriage ranged from tightly curled over the back to a low carriage. The early German Shepherd Dog's form followed his function; in other words, his size, shape, and movement were

only thought of if it enabled the dog to perform the functions of his job better.

The German Shepherd Dog as a Versatile Herding Dog

By the late 1800s, the form and function of the German Shepherd Dog had taken shape as three distinct types. In the Wurttenberg region, the shepherds in the area had a beautifully set, low tail and came in a variety of colors. Shepherding dogs from the Thuringia area had the highly desirable, erect, wolflike ears; however, not surprisingly, they were predominantly wolf gray. And in Swabia, the regional shepherds were renowned for their herding abilites, and they were agile with great strength, speed, and endurance.

One individual, Max von Stephanitz, worked with breeders from the three areas. And, from 1889 to 1899 he created what was to become the purebred German Shepherd Dog.

War Dog

Max von Stephanitz, the founder of what would become Germany's German Shepherd Dog club, Verein für Deutsche Schäferhunde, felt that the German Shepherd Dog was capable of much more than its current service as a versatile herding dog. Von Stephanitz, who was a captain in the German Army's cavalry, recognized the GSD's potential as a military and/or a police dog. He was correct, as the German Shepherd Dog had already per-

Three Purposes, Three Bites

From the combined duty of herding, farm work, and guarding sheep, the GSD developed three basic types of bites. The first is the herding nip, in which the dog nips at the hocks of the sheep and lambs to encourage them to move in a certain direction (away from him, typically). The nips do not break the skin and are delivered with just enough pressure to encourage the flock to move forward.

The second type of bite is what is referred to as a "grab and hold." The German Shepherd Dog uses this when a sheep or lamb is in immediate danger and must be moved right away. No harm is meant by the grab and hold, rather the dog uses just enough force to grasp the leg of the lamb or sheep and pull it out of danger. If the lamb or sheep struggles, the grasp becomes firmer, but again, it is never meant to injure the animal.

The third type of bite is "reactive." This bite is meant to do damage, and it is reserved for predators, poachers, or other perceived dangers to the flock. The German Shepherd Dog gives the predator or poacher plenty of warning with body language—growling, snarling, and barking—that the option of "flight" is not going to be chosen over "fight." Even with this third type of bite, the GSD was never bred to bite in an uncontrolled frenzy but rather just to ward off evil. He has the courage to fight if needed.

formed valiantly as a sentry, a messenger dog, and a carrier of medical supplies during Prussian times.

During World War I, the British, French, and German armies trained and used German Shepherd Dogs in military service. Post-World War I proved nearly fatal for the breed, as not only thousands of dogs were killed in service but also many notable GSD breeders were killed in the war, too. The great famine in Germany that occurred after WWI, as well as the scarcity of veterinary care and medicine, caused a great many more dogs to die. And, many of the dogs that the famine didn't kill ultimately perished from the rampant spread of canine diseases.

Yet, breeders in Great Britain, the United States, Germany, and many European countries worked diligently to restore the breed's numbers.

When it became evident that World War II was imminent, many German breeders sought to save their German Shepherd Dogs that they had worked so hard to bring back. Some breeders shipped their dogs out of the country. Others, who lived in the city and remembered the difficulties of the famine following WWI, sent their dogs to relatives and friends who lived on farms in the hopes that their dogs could survive in an area with ample food. And, others reportedly euthanized their prized dogs as an alternative to death on the battle field or the slow starvation in a soon-to-be war-torn country.

At the beginning of WWII, Germany had an estimated 200,000 war dogs, with the majority of those being German Shepherd Dogs.

In the United States, more than 30 breeds were initially used for military work, but by the end of 1942, only five breeds were recommended for war dog work, with the German Shepherd Dog heading the list.

WWII war dog tasks were similar to those in WWI: patrol, sentry, medic, and messenger. Additionally, war dogs had some unusual jobs, such as those that were attached to British parachute battalions and were referred to as "para pups." Brian, a German Shepherd Dog attached to one such parachute battalion, was awarded the Dickin Medal for gallantry and devotion to duty. The German Shepherd Dog made and survived the landing in Normandy and became a fully-qualified paratrooper based on the number of jumps he made.

War Dog Jobs

Military dogs have performed a vast array of jobs while serving over the past century. Some of the earliest jobs, in which GSDs participated and excelled, include the following.

Sentry The sentry dog worked closely with his handler and warned of the approach or presence of a person. Of the 10,425 dogs employed in WWII, 9,300 were used for sentry work. Sentry dogs often patrolled airports, supply depots,

No Dog Left Behind

A distressing part of U.S. military dog history occurred in 1975, at the end of the U.S.'s involvement in the Vietnam War. When troops were returning home from Vietnam, their dogs were not allowed to return with them, leaving more than 1,000 dogs. (The U.S. Marine Corps is the exception; risking punishment, dog handlers worked to find ways to get their dogs home.) The forced abandonment of military working dogs in Vietnam affected dog handlers so profoundly, that handlers worked together to successfully change this policy, and now the motto is uniformly, "No Dog Left Behind."

arsenals, and vital installations. More than 3,000 dogs were trained and issued to the Coast Guard in 1943 for beach patrols and to guard against enemy submarine activities.

Patrol/Scout The patrol or scout dog was trained to work and silently signal (e.g., raised hair, stiffened body, rigid tail) his handler when he detected enemy forces, snipers, and/or an ambush. Often walking in front of combat and infantry patrols, the patrol dog and his handler not only saved many lives but also boosted morale among units. It is reported that scout dogs detected the enemy up to 1,000 yards away.

Messenger Messenger dogs typically worked with two handlers and silently navigated rough and difficult terrain to send and deliver messages between the handlers.

Mine Detection The "M-Dog" was trained to find not only metallic and non-metallic mines, but also trip wires and booby traps. Today, the Army has MDDs (Mine Detection Dogs) that work slowly and methodically off-leash for buried mines and/or artillery. German Shepherd Dogs are used for this work, as well as Labrador retrievers and Belgian Malinois.

Casualty Dogs Also known as medic dogs and comfort dogs (depending on the country they were serving), these dogs were trained much like Search and Rescue (SAR) dogs in that they worked in the battlefield to find injured, living soldiers. When the dogs found injured soldiers, they were trained to run back to their handlers and then lead their handlers (medics) to the injured.

Tunnel Dogs During the Vietnam War, the Viet Cong would hide in small, dark tunnels underground that were treacherous for soldiers to navigate. Dogs were trained to detect the hidden entries to the tunnels and explore the tunnels for dwellers, who greatly feared the dogs.

Bloodhounds

The first use of dogs specifically for law enforcement dates back to the Middle Ages when bloodhounds were used in England, France, and Scotland to track down outlaws.

Sled and Pack These dogs did exactly what it sounds like: carried packs and pulled sleds filled with equipment.

Modern Day Military Dog Jobs

Explosives Detection In today's war on terrorism, there is a significant threat of explosives hidden on a person or in a vehicle or planted at a roadside location. Explosives also are stored in secret caches. Explosive Detection Dogs (EDDs) are trained to alert to all forms of explosives, which can then be disarmed or disposed of by an Explosive Ordinance Disposal (EOD) unit. A division of EDDs are the Specialized Search Dogs (SSDs) that work at long distances from their handlers and through hand signals. SSDs that work in the Marine Corps are trained to take commands through a radio that is worn on the dogs' backs. SSDs are usually German Shepherd Dogs.

IED Detector Dogs and Tactical Explosive Detector Dogs (TEDDs) These specialized detection dogs search for Improvised Explosive Devices (IEDs). Both IED Dogs and TEDDs were originally formed as a temporary program to fill an urgent need for highly-trained dogs that could safely detect IEDs. The IED Dogs program is run by the Marine Corps; the TEDD program is run by the Army.

Combat Tracking The Combat Tracker Dog (CTD) is trained to track down people who have hidden or laid explosives. CTDs are Marine Corps dogs. Typically, the breeds that are chosen for CTD work are also those that are trained for dual-purpose work, such as German or Dutch Shepherd Dogs and Belgian Malinois.

With changing wars came changing purposes. Today's military dogs continue to serve as sentry and patrol dogs, as well as many additional duties; however, one of the most popular breeds for all ranges of military work remains the German Shepherd Dog.

Police K-9s

The history of the German Shepherd Dog as a police dog dates as far back, if not farther, than the GSDs service in military work. A police department in Ghent, Belgium is credited with creating the first organized police dog training program in 1895. From Belgium, the training methods (mostly for patrol work) spread to England, Austria, Hungary, and Germany. In 1920, the German police opened their first police dog training school in Greenheide.

Meanwhile, from 1907–1918, the United States initiated a police dog program in New York that allowed pet dogs to roam freely with officers on patrol.

It was not until the 1970s, however, that police dogs were more widely used—the German Shepherd Dog being one of the most popular choices for police departments. Police dogs were reportedly being used as patrol dogs in approximately 80 departments across the

Search and Rescue (SAR)

GSDs have long been a favorite for SAR work, both with volunteer SAR and police K-9s. German Shepherd Dogs have a double coat that protects them from the elements, such as dense briars and brush commonly encountered in searches. The best SAR German Shepherd Dogs have an unending energy supply, which is needed for long searches in difficult terrain. German Shepherd Dogs are also quick and can cover a lot of ground in a very short amount of time. And, of course, the ability to think independently, coupled with a high working drive, makes GSDs stellar search and rescue dogs.

United States, including major cities where crime had been escalating, such as St. Louis, Washington, D.C., Chicago, Philadelphia, and Miami.

Police dogs advanced in their required skill sets over the next 30 years and now include: pursuit, narcotics and explosives detection, evidence discovery, and search and rescue. Depending on the needs of the department, dogs may be dual purpose (i.e., pursuit and nar-

cotics) or single purpose, such as explosives detection. The German Shepherd Dog remains one of the most popular choices as a multipurpose police dog.

Service Dogs

Though records indicate that dogs were used to assist the blind as early as 79 A.D. in Pompeii, it wasn't until centuries later that dogs were considered for formal training as guide dogs for the blind. And, the dog of choice was the German Shepherd Dog.

The individual credited with the beginning of the GSD's service with the blind is Dr. Gerhard Stalling, a German physician from World War I. During World War I, many German soldiers were returning from the front, blinded from mustard gas exposure or the result of shell shock. Dr. Stalling, who often had his GSD with him, left his German Shepherd Dog with a blind patient at the hospital while he attended to an urgent matter elsewhere. When he returned, the GSD was assisting the patient. Dr. Stalling, aware of the work the ambulance/comfort dogs were performing in the war, felt that he could train GSDs to assist blinded veterans. In August of 1916, he opened what would be the world's first guide dog school for the blind in Oldenburg, Germany.

The school grew to add several additional training branches in Bonn, Breslau, Dresden, Essen, Freiburg, Hamburg, Magdeburg, Munster, and Hanover. The centers at their peak were producing 600 trained GSD guide dogs annually.

In 1923, the German Shepherd Dog Association took over training guide dogs for the blind and opened a training school in Potsdam. It is here that the basis was formed for many of the training concepts used by guide dog schools today—specifically in puppy selection, in-home puppy rearing, and matching trained dogs to owners.

In 1929, The Seeing Eye organization was founded in Nashville, Tennessee (later relocated to New Jersey). Today, the breeds used by The Seeing Eye still include the German Shepherd Dog, along with Labrador Retrievers and Golden Retrievers, and a Lab/Golden cross for prospective Seeing Eye dogs.

After decades of successful use as guide dogs for the blind, interest grew in how dogs could be used for other disabilities, and the GSD continued to be a top choice for service dog work. By the 1960s, dogs assisting people with disabilities became more widespread in the United States.

Today, GSDs still actively work as the following:

- Guide dogs for the blind
- Autism service dogs (dog lowers incidences of volatile behaviors by calming patient; creates safety for family members)
- Hearing assistance dogs (alert to noises, such as the front door, telephone, and dangers, such as fire)

- Seizure alert dogs (alert to "aura" prior to a seizure) and diabetic awareness dogs (alert to the change in breath)
- Medical alert dogs (can be trained to alert to a variety of conditions, such as heart attack, stroke, diabetes, epilepsy, etc.)
- Mobility dogs (tasks ranging from picking up keys and credit cards to opening doors and pushing elevator buttons for those in wheelchairs, to assisting with balance for those with some mobility, and much more)
- Post Traumatic Stress Disorder (PTSD) dogs (trained primarily for veterans having difficulty handling anxiety, nightmares, panic attacks, etc., but also for first responders and civilians suffering from the effects of a traumatic event)

Therapy Dogs

Although German Shepherd Dogs (along with other breeds) have been used unofficially for therapeutic purposes and companionship since the breed was first developed, it wasn't until 1976 that the therapeutic effects of dogs on humans was recorded. Elaine Smith, RN, is credited with creating a systematic approach to the training and use of therapy dogs with patients. Among other physiological effects, Smith noted that dogs could help patients by lowering blood pressure, providing stress relief, raising morale, as well as helping to overcome psychological disorders.

In 1982, Nancy Stanley of La Costa, California founded Tender Loving Zoo. She introduced therapy dogs to severely disabled children and researched the dogs' effects on the children. Stanley is considered the pioneer of today's therapy dogs.

Therapy dogs are required to have a Canine Good Citizen title (see pages 143–144), as well as a passing score on a test specifically tailored for certifying therapy dog teams (you and your dog) by a recognized therapy dog institution, such as Therapy Dogs International. Although virtually any dog can be a therapy dog if he has the correct temperament and training, the well-balanced, well-socialized German Shepherd Dog can and does make an excellent therapy dog.

Therapy dogs are classified in three different categories: Therapeutic Visitation Dogs, Animal-Assisted Therapy Dogs, and Facility Therapy Dogs.

Therapeutic Visitation Dogs are those dogs that work with their handler as a team in hospitals, nursing homes, rehabilitation centers, and schools for reading programs. These dogs assist in providing comfort in post-traumatic situations, such as after 9-11, natural disasters (hurricane or tornado stricken areas), and visiting with military members post-deployment. Therapeutic Visitation Dogs also work in Child Advocacy Centers, assisting in calming abused children and to calm child witnesses in courtrooms.

Animal-Assisted Therapy (AAT) dogs work with patients in patient care programs, typically along with physical therapists and occupational therapists. AAT Dogs may assist patients with fine-motor control, gaining motion in limbs, and even walking.

Facility Therapy Dogs are a little different because these dogs live in the facility where they work and are handled by trained staff members. These types of dogs are seen primarily in Alzheimer's or dementia wards, and their primary purpose is to keep patients from endangering themselves.

By law, service dogs, therapy dogs, and emotional support dogs

Emotional Support Dog

An emotional support dog is one that provides companionship, comfort, and therapeutic benefits to you. Although the emotional support dog plays an important role in your mental health, he is *not* a therapy dog or a service dog.

each have different rights as to where they can be taken, including public places and public transportation, as well as where they can live. Service dogs—those that are trained specifically to perform multiple tasks for a disabled individual—are allowed to work wherever the disabled person needs to be. Therapy dogs do not have this privilege nor do emotional support dogs. Be aware, too, that more states are penalizing dog owners who falsely claim their dogs are service dogs when they are actually pets.

Characteristics and Drives

So, knowing the German Shepherd Dog's long history of herding, military, police, service, and therapy work, it is obvious that this breed has exceptionally varied skills and is truly a versatile dog. What does this mean to you, however, the one who is training him to be a good companion? Realizing the characteristics and drives that make the GSD the versatile dog he is today will help you to understand why he displays certain behaviors and how best to channel those behaviors and drives.

Herding Tendencies The German Shepherd Dog was first and foremost a versatile herding dog. He can still herd today, and the breed regularly competes in herding trials. Natural herding tendencies mean the GSD will want to gather whatever he deems as his flock. If he is unable to move all his "flock" (which for him could mean anyone in the home) into one location, it could result in nervous pacing or the inability to be still or relax. These strong herding instincts can result in unwanted herding of children and other pets,

which may include nipping and grab-and-pull herding maneuvers.

Watchdog Abilities The GSD was bred to be alert to changes in his environment, and as such he has a keen ability to detect movement and subtle differences in his environment. The GSD was bred to respond with barking, growling, etc., until the perceived threat either leaves or is determined not to be a danger. Good socialization is the key to help him determine the difference between honest threats and friendly encounters. Also, keen watchdog abilities translate to the potential for much unwanted vocalization; GSDs are very vocal, and can not only bark a lot but also whine, cry, and otherwise voice their concerns.

Protective Instincts The German Shepherd Dog was bred to be a multipurpose herding dog, not only to herd sheep, but to protect his flock *and family* as well. He was raised to protect his flock from *big* predators—wolves, bears, and armed people. Throughout history, the German Shepherd Dog is known not only for his gentleness (with his flock and family) but also for his ability to be a fierce protector. What this means to you is that it is critical that he sees kind, gentle people as exactly that—not a threat. If the GSD is not socialized with people and other dogs and animals, he can become overly protective—both of your home (his territory) and you. Additionally, as a protective dog, he is very sensitive to your anxieties and will look for the cause of your ner-

vousness. He is *not* the dog for a meek or easily frightened person, as he will fall into the role of protecting the person against *everyone and everything*, making him overly protective and a possible liability.

High Prey/Play Drive High prey/play drive dogs will work endlessly for balls, tug toys, and other items. If the dog is from working lines (see "Three Types of German Shepherd Dogs," page 20), he will have an exceptionally high prey/play drive, as this is what makes him such a great herding and working dog—he will work endlessly for rewards. This drive is one of the reasons the GSD is sought after as a working dog, service dog, and performance event dog. The prey/play drive is an essential tool in training dogs. But, it can also mean that he will play with balls,

toys, tugs, and other items *endlessly* in your home, and he will want you to be a constant and committed playmate.

High Activity Level Working dogs have high activity levels because they were bred to work all day. Herding dogs often have an even higher activity level, as they were bred to work all day with many high bursts of speed. The German Shepherd Dog is an active dog; if he comes from true working lines, his activity level will be even higher. If you plan on working your dog, competing in performance events, or are a very active individual who will be taking your GSD everywhere, you may still have difficulties meeting his higher exercise needs. Long walks alone may not suffice, and even daily hard runs may only take the

edge off your dog. And, a German Shepherd Dog with pent up energy is a destructive dog.

Three Types of German Shepherd Dogs

Working/Performance Lines GSDs from working and/or performance lines are those that are bred specifically to work as military or police K-9s; to serve in some branch of government, such as the Transportation Security Administration (TSA), Border Patrol, FBI, etc.; to compete in performance events (such as schutzhund, agility, tracking, etc.); and to work as Search and Rescue dogs. These lines are bred for high prey/play drives and correct structure, and they typically come from European lines. Working/performance lines are usually very healthy, intelligent, and of sound temperament; however, because of the exceptionally high prey/play drive, coupled with a tireless activity level, these dogs do not make good household pets for the novice owner. With this said, the experienced, quality breeder will know if there is a puppy in a litter that is not as intense as his littermates, and this pup could make a very good companion dog.

Show Lines Bred with a more extremely sloped topline (the line of the dog's back from shoulder to the base of the tail), these dogs maintain the same basic drives as the working/performance lines, though they are generally not as intense. Show lines breed for conformation, health, and temperament—those that aren't reserved for showing (i.e., "pet quality") can make great companions.

Backyard Dogs Unfortunately, this type of GSD makes up the majority of puppies that are available and advertised. They are either accidentally bred or they are bred for money. The "breeder" may have good intentions; however, the mated dogs are rarely temperament tested. So, puppies are more likely to have poor temperaments (aggressive or timid) and often have poor "nerves," leading them to such behaviors as tail chasing, chewing on their own tails, and licking granulomas (an area of exposed, red skin and raw areas on the lower extremities caused by excessive licking). Additionally, the mated dogs are rarely, if ever, health tested for chronic or potentially fatal diseases with a genetic component, such as chronic and costly skin allergies, debilitating Canine Hip Dysplasia, and a blinding and sometimes painful eye disease.

Can you find a healthy, calm, intelligent GSD with a rock solid temperament from a backyard-bred litter? Yes. But, because these GSDs were not bred by an experienced, quality breeder, it can be more difficult to find a good pup.

It is important to note that rescued German Shepherd Dogs—those GSDs that wound up in a shelter or a rescue—come from all three types of breeders noted above: working/performance, show, and backyard breeders. The reason they are relinquished is usually no fault of their own; they were just being GSDs and it is likely that their exercise, leadership, training, and mental stimulation requirements were not being met.

Intensity of Focus

The GSD can focus at a younger age than other breeds, which means you can begin training as soon as you bring him home, and he will be able to retain that training. The ability for him to focus on tasks at such an early age can also work against you, in that he can be very focused on getting what he wants, such as opening a cabinet door, letting himself out, climbing up onto tables and counters, or even escaping from the backyard. In a perfect world, you would channel your pup's ability to focus as a young puppy and would have him well trained before he got big enough to push his weight around, or before his hormones kick in at around six or seven months of age.

Independent Thinker

The German Shepherd Dog is a rather unique blend of both a working/follow orders type of dog and a dog that was bred to think independently and take the actions he feels are necessary to perform his duties. The German Shepherd Dog, therefore, is comfortable working directly with his handler as well as working at a distance and making decisions independently. With the German Shepherd Dog, it is more about *when* (not *if*) the independent streak comes up in training—when your GSD thinks he knows best. If you have used good training techniques, worked diligently with your dog, and have established

a solid leadership role, the German Shepherd Dog's independent thinking will not cause any issues. Even if he momentarily questions your command, he will willingly follow your lead.

Excellent Sense of Smell

German Shepherd Dogs are recognized for their scenting and tracking ability. With training, the GSD can excel not only in tracking (following a human's scent), trailing (following a human's scent and identifying that person), but also in scent discrimination exercises. The German Shepherd Dog is considered one of the world's top Search and Rescue dogs because of his scenting ability combined with his size and athleticism. How does this translate to the GSD as a pet in the

home? You can never "hide" anything in your home. He will find it, particularly if it is edible or if it's his favorite ball. He will be *relentless* in his work to find the desired object.

Strength

Bred to excel in work that requires not only strength and endurance but agility as well, the German Shepherd Dog is an amazing dog to watch when in motion and at work. With that said, the GSD's strength can work against you if you don't train him in the basics at an early age. You will experience his strength as he pulls you down the street, knocks down visitors in your home, or as you try to get him to go to his crate. A full-grown GSD cannot (and should not) be physically forced to do anything he doesn't want to do, which is why using positive training techniques is key for all ages of the German Shepherd Dog. By doing so, it will allow you to train him without ever having to confront his strength.

Courage

A well-bred GSD will have courage. Courage is not aggression. Courage is the kind, gentle, friendly, obedient German Shepherd Dog that when called to do something potentially dangerous or treacherous, will respond without hesitation and with full effort. Courage is displayed in protecting flocks from predators, tracking a person through rough terrain, navigating a vision-impaired individual through a crossing during rush hour, and remaining calm when a dementia patient begins screaming nonsensically at the dog. How does courage affect your training? Your German Shepherd Dog will not be intimidated by you or respect harsh training methods. He is a willing, eager student, but he will not tolerate poor treatment.

Hormonal Drives

The GSD begins to realize hormonal drives around six to seven months of age. In some dogs, this change in hormones can create a less trainable and more challenging, in-your-face kind of dog. Spay/neuter will change the unwanted, fractious, and pushy behaviors that stem from hormones, almost immediately upon altering the dog. Altering your German Shepherd Dog will *not* change his temperament or overall "personality," but it *will* stop the dog's unwanted behaviors that stem from his or her hormones.

How Challenging Will This Training Journey Be?

The GSD puppy comes to you bright, joyful, and eager to learn. What you do with him, how you train

Early Spay/Neuter Concerns

The current thought on spaying or neutering the GSD is that waiting until the dog is two years old helps prevent such health-related issues as musculoskeletal disorders in both sexes and urinary incontinence in female dogs.

If your GSD is *not* showing any unwanted behaviors and/or not displaying any forms of aggression (see *Aggression* chapter, pages 127–141), then your veterinarian may advise you to wait until your GSD is two years old before you spay or neuter.

If your GSD *is* showing unwanted behaviors, constantly challenging you, or displaying any early signs of aggression, spay or neuter immediately before these behaviors have a chance to worsen. Balancing behaviors versus overall health of the dog is a decision not to be taken lightly; however, making the decision to better the dog's behavior should always take priority, as if bad behaviors turn ugly, the health your dog has in five years won't matter anymore because you won't have the dog anymore.

him, what environmental factors you expose him to, and what skills you teach him will greatly impact how easy and enjoyable your training journey will be. For the vast majority of puppy owners, training your

German Shepherd Dog will be fun and immensely rewarding.

If you wait until he has reached adolescence before beginning his training, you will have more challenges because you have left his "training" up to him for his first several months on this earth. This could mean that you and your GSD must really focus on training and make a very serious and consistent effort to bring him up-to-speed and back on the training track. Once he's caught up, you will also realize that, along the way, you and your German Shepherd Dog had fun and that this training stuff works.

If you are working with a young adult coming out of a German Shepherd Dog rescue or shelter, the training needs of your rescue may be simple, or they could be more challenging (see "Working with the Rescued German Shepherd Dog," page 32). Training a rescued GSD requires knowledge of the dog's current abilities, as well as his quirks, fears, or any tendencies toward aggression and/ or dominance. If you are

working with a reputable GSD rescue, or one of many full-service shelters, the German Shepherd Dog will have been thoroughly temperament tested and vetted as to his abilities to live with other pets and small children. Adopting a GSD out of an animal control center with limited funding and even more limited abilities to analyze dogs at intake will require an experienced German Shepherd Dog owner and trainer to determine the level of training the dog will need to succeed.

One common denominator— regardless of the age of the German Shepherd Dog—is that along your training journey, you will increase your training skills and your ability to understand and know your German Shepherd Dog. He *will* learn and he will become as trained and obedient as you want him to be. If you are kind and consistent in your training and you provide your GSD with a solid leader (you), he will be your loyal, trusted friend and faithful companion.

Chapter Three

German Shepherd Dog Training 101

Approach to Training

Whether you are new to dog training or an old hand, the approach taken toward training dogs has evolved over the past several decades. Today, nearly all trainers are on-board with positive reinforcement, reward-based training, which makes training much more fun for the dog and handler, and equally, if not more, effective than previous methods that involved harsh, physical punishments.

The Power of Positive Reinforcement

Positive reinforcement training rewards the dog when he does something right. The reward for doing something correctly can be verbal praise, physical praise (rubs and pats), a toy or a treat. (For more information on rewards, see "Reinforcements: What They Are and How They Work," pages 88–89.) Positive reinforcement training sets the dog up for success as the exer-

cises are set up to take small steps (that can be rewarded) to achieve a much bigger behavior. The process of building smaller behaviors and rewarding the dog along the way helps to create greater trust and a deeper bond between the dog and handler. Dogs learn just as quickly and reliably with positive reinforcement training as they did in previous eras with negative reinforcement training. The biggest difference is that the final, trained dog is a much more joyful and enthusiastic training partner than the dog that was trained using exclusively negative reinforcement training.

Learning Capabilities of the Puppy, Adolescent, and Adult

What can your German Shepherd Dog learn and when does he learn it? The following is a guideline as to the learning capabilities of your GSD from puppyhood to adulthood, as well as some critical time periods in which the GSD is most impressionable.

Ages 0 to 7 Weeks: Neonatal, Transition, Awareness, and Canine Socialization. During this period, the puppy is with his mother and littermates. The puppy's mother and littermates teach the puppy about social interaction, play, and inhibiting aggression This is the critical time period in which the puppy learns appropriate dog behaviors and how to interact with other dogs.

Ages 7 to 14 Weeks: Human Socialization Period. The puppy now has the brain waves of an adult dog, but his attention span is short. This period is when the most rapid learning occurs. Learning at this age is permanent, so this is a perfect time to start training. Also, this is the ideal time to introduce the puppy to things that will play an important part in his life. Introduce the puppy to different people, places, animals, and sounds in a positive, non-threatening way. For more information on socializing with people, see pages 56–62.

Early Separation Issues

Puppies that are separated from their mother and littermates before they reach eight weeks of age are in jeopardy of developing into adolescents and adult GSDs that may be more problematic in accepting leadership from their owners. In fact, most conscientious breeders keep the puppies together with their littermates and in continued contact with the mother until the puppies are at least nine weeks old.

Keeping puppies with their mother and littermates has been recognized as critically important to the point at which some states have enacted laws that puppies cannot be sold before they've reached eight weeks of age.

Ages 8 to 10/11 Weeks: Fear Imprint Period. Avoid frightening the puppy during this period. The reasons for this "fear imprint period" are not clearly understood; however, it is known that any traumatic, frightening, or painful experience that the puppy experiences during this two- to three-week period will have a more lasting effect on the

puppy than if it occurred at any other time in its life.

Ages 13 to 16 Weeks: Seniority Classification Period or "The Age of Cutting." This is the four-week period in which the puppy cuts his teeth and his apron strings! Teething means your GSD puppy will want to chew all the time and on everything he can get his teeth on. When puppy teeth fall out and the adult teeth erupt, the puppy is very uncomfortable and chewing and gnawing helps ease his discomfort. It is very important to give your pup good, healthy toys and chews to satisfy his need to chew; however, it is also important that your puppy clearly understands that chewing on you or your family members is not accept-able. Remember, your puppy is now beginning to test who is going to make the rules in the home. With no rules, a dog will make his own rules, and you don't want to live by those. One of the ways a puppy—and an older dog—establishes a pecking order (or tries to enforce his rules) includes biting, in addition to a myriad of other unwanted behaviors. For this reason, it is important that—even though your GSD is little and has little teeth—you don't promote or encourage biting.

Ages 4 to 8 Months: Play Instinct and Flight Instinct Period. When your GSD puppy hits four months old, he begins to wander and ignore you. He also gains a strong play instinct, which is often a

giant game of keep-away from *you* and if he's not on leash, you won't be able to catch him. Additionally, this is the period in which he experiences a flight instinct period: If he is startled or frightened, he will take off running.

For this reason, it is very important that you keep the puppy on a leash at this time. Additionally, the way you handle the puppy determines if he will come to you when called. Your GSD puppy will continue to lose his milk teeth and break in his adult teeth for a few months. (A dog's teeth don't set in his jaw until between six and ten months.) During this time, your puppy is also enter-

ing puberty and a dog that has a propensity to be pushy may start to exhibit these behaviors now, and that includes using his mouth in less innocuous ways. Again, do not allow any chewing on people.

Ages 6 to 14 Months: Second Fear Imprint Period or Fear of New Situations Period. During these eight months, your GSD may again show fear of new situations and even familiar situations. You may find your GSD is suddenly reluctant to approach someone or something new. It is important that you are patient and act very matter-of-fact in these situations. Never force the dog to face the situation. DO NOT pet the frightened puppy or talk in soothing tones. The puppy will interpret such responses as praise for being frightened. Training will help improve the dog's confidence, as it deepens the bond between the dog and handler and, as a result, increases the dog's trust in the handler. He looks more and more to his owner. Agility is one of the top recommended activities for dogs and owners to increase a dog's confidence with all sorts of situations. It's a positive, rewarding activity that is fun for both dog and owner and can build even a fearful dog's confidence.

Ages 1 to 4 Years: Maturity Period. If your GSD is an intact male dog (or less commonly, an intact female dog) that is driven by hormones, you could see an increase in attempts to "get his/her way" or pushy behaviors during this time period. If you have spent considerable time training your dog, and thereby have established a healthy dog-owner relationship in which he looks to you for guidance, rules, and fun (because training is fun!), then you should be well on your way to raising a wonderful canine companion. If hormonal pushiness becomes a larger issue, altering your dog during this time period is an option.

Ages 12 to 16 months of age: Another Fear Imprint Period (Possibly). This is another time period in which your GSD may be either more sensitive to frighten-

ing experiences or may show (again) fear of a new or an accustomed situation. As with the other two fear imprint stages, you want to be careful as to how you respond to your GSDs fear reaction by not "soothing" him but rather acting confident and patient, and do not force any interaction with anything that frightens him. (For more on how to handle this, see pages 56–62.)

Home Schooling: Working with the Rescued German Shepherd Dog

German Shepherd Dogs do not usually wind up in rescue without some sort of problem behavior; there is a reason they have been given up to rescue. Many GSDs that find themselves in a shelter or a rescue situation may need socialization with people or dogs or both. Others may have anxiety issues. And, still others may have had no training at all and have developed bad behaviors.

The positive news is that if a GSD has found a place in a good shelter, animal rescue, or a breed rescue that fully evaluates dogs at intake and/or while being fostered, adopting a GSD just got much easier. Well-run shelters and animal or breed rescues that have the resources to evaluate GSDs and *know* the breed well, will know not only if a particular GSD has issues, but what those issues are and how best to deal with those issues. Many well-funded shelters, animal rescues, and breed rescues will also pay to bring the GSD up-to-date with his vaccinations, correct or begin treating any health issues, and complete a spay/neuter. Additionally, these organizations will work to determine how the GSD is with other dogs, people, children, home noises, etc.

The potential bad news, however, is that if you are adopting a GSD from an organization with minimal resources (i.e., no fostering, no in-depth behavioral analysis, no modification training, etc.), you won't know what behavioral issues your adopted GSD may or may not have. GSDs notoriously do not do well in a noisy, crowded shelter environment, which may suppress their worst behaviors. Conversely, the GSD may present super-aggressive behaviors in the shelter that are *not* typical for him, nor representative of his character. For the latter dog, when he is in a foster home that is quiet and not populated with barking, crying dogs, he will likely exhibit his true, calm behavior. If you adopt out of a shelter or rescue that does not temperament test, proceed with **extreme** caution. Preferably, enlist an experienced working dog trainer, a longtime GSD owner, or a trusted veterinarian to assist you in evaluating the GSD.

If you do bring home a rescue/shelter dog that has not been evaluated by a skilled trainer, an animal behaviorist, or someone experienced with rescuing GSDs and other working breed dogs, be particularly careful with the following:

- Any children in the house *must* have appropriate dog manners (see "Rules for Children," page 59).
- The dog *must* have 24-hour supervision when with children. Never leave the dog alone with your children or grandchildren, no matter how good the dog appears to be or how well-behaved you think the children are. The perfect storm for a potentially trau-

matic or even disfiguring accident is exactly at this time: when a dog (especially one that you do not know what his triggers are—a sound, a noise, or even touching a particularly sensitive part on his body) is left unsupervised with children. (Training *needs* to begin the day the dog comes home; not a couple of weeks later.)

- The rescued dog must understand that the children are part of the family and not his to boss around—which can be done gently and effectively with obedience training and exercises to increase the dog's trust and devotion to his new family.

If you are introducing the new GSD to a dog or dogs already in your home, care must also be taken. For the initial introduction, follow the procedures outlined in "Socialization with Dogs," on pages 62–65. When in the home, make sure you provide 24/7 supervision for the new rescue and the home's resident dog(s). If you can't supervise, separate. Keep toys, treats, and any potential high-value items away from all dogs when they are together, and make sure to provide the resident dog(s) with additional attention so that this new situation is viewed as a positive one.

Training the rescued GSD is similar to beginning training with any adult GSD, but in this case you must rely more heavily on the GSD Rescue's (or an experienced GSD trainer's) evaluation of the dog. It is also critically important to begin the dog's training

the moment he comes home and not wait for him to "settle in" to his new surroundings. If you wait for the dog to settle in, he will have time to evaluate his surroundings and size you up. When he's comfortable (1 to 2 months later) and knows what the household is like, then he will go back to his bad behaviors and you will have an even bigger mess. So, rule number one: Start training the moment his paws set down in your home.

The second rule is to teach him to *focus* (see pages 95–97). He needs to learn to look to you and to keep his attention on you and what you want him to do.

Along with teaching him *focus*, also begin teaching the basics of the *sit, down, stay,* and *leave it* commands *before* he gets back in his groove and starts behaving badly.

It is important to use the reward system in training and to lure him into positions (see pages 86–87). Luring allows you to achieve the behavior you want without ever touching him, which can be a stressor or a trigger in some dogs that have been badly handled previously, that have a hidden injury, or that have had little to no handling in the past.

For the lure, you will want to find what he likes more than anything else and use this to help teach him commands.

Finally, you will want your adopted GSD to realize that he is required to do *something* for every reward he gets, as this will gently establish leadership.

Chapter Four
Housetraining

One of the most appreciated aspects of owning a GSD—whether a puppy, an adult dog, or an age in between, is that the German Shepherd Dog is a very easy dog to housetrain. He is smart, wants to learn, and with consistency and training, his ability to learn to relieve himself outside is fairly remarkable.

The key to making his housetraining go smoothly is to understand your GSD's urges and abilities, and to use these to shape the housetraining behaviors you want. This is true whether you are working with a little puppy or an older GSD that hasn't had any previous housetraining.

The techniques and methods used in training a puppy are a little different than housetraining an adult dog; however, the principles are basically the same—it's the ability of the dog to "hold" that is different. So, let's start off with housetraining the little ones.

Your Pup's Urges and Abilities

By nature, your GSD puppy will want to keep his space clean. This is an "urge" that is primarily genetic, as once pups are big enough to start walking and their eyes are open, they will naturally relieve themselves away from their mother and the source of their food. With this said, when you bring your eight-week-old puppy home, his initial idea of "space" and yours may be vastly different. For example, if you have him in an adult size crate, he may think he has plenty of room to relieve himself in one corner and sleep in another.

His idea of what is "enough" space will increase with age and as he increases in size. So, as a pup, it could be the corner of a large crate; as an older puppy, the corner of the kitchen may be far enough away; and as an adult, he may think that a room off the hall will be far enough from his living area that it's okay to defecate there. Of course, it's not. This is where your housetraining efforts will come into play.

As your puppy gets older, his ability to "hold" will increase. A good way to estimate how long your GSD can reasonably "hold" is relative to his age. At eight weeks old, he should be able to rest quietly in his crate for about two hours—if he has

The No Scolding Rule

Owners often will claim that they can tell if their dogs have done something "bad" by their demeanor. This is wrong. The so-called bad dog "guilty" behaviors are actually the behaviors a dog would exhibit naturally—without knowing why—when his owner's body language, voice, and other cues indicate that the owner is angry.

If you want to test this theory out, act happy, put a pep in your step, and use a higher voice when talking with your dog after you've spotted an "accident." Your GSD won't act "guilty" at all. Why? He will act just as peppy because he is responding to your joyfulness.

Scolding a dog "after the fact" is not an effective housetraining method. In fact, it can destroy some of the good training you've invested in him. For example, if you call him over to you after you've spotted an accident, and he comes happily to you, at which time you grab his collar and thoroughly

scold him for the accident, here is what you've taught him:

- If he comes to you when you call him, you will punish him, so don't come when you're called!
- If you grab him by the collar, something bad is going to happen, so stay out of reach!

When can you scold a dog that has an accident? The only time an "Ah-Ah" might be permissible is if you see your pup *in the act of relieving himself*, and then the words "Ah-Ah" can be used in an attempt to startle the pup and possibly stop the stream as you whisk him outside (without malice!).

Remember, if he has an accident it is your fault because you either didn't see the warning signs, you left him alone too long, you gave him too much "space" too quickly, or one of many other reasons.

So, if he has an accident, clean it up and figure out what went wrong and how you can make it easier for your GSD to not have an accident in the future.

had the opportunity to relieve himself right before he was put in the crate and if he is calm and relaxed when in the crate.

At four months of age, the pup should be able to hold for four hours at a time. At six months of age, he can "hold" for up to six hours, and by eight months of age, he should be able to "hold" overnight. Of

course, these times will vary according to the pup, but as a rule, if the pup has relieved himself before being put in the crate, and he is calm and resting, these time frames are good guidelines to use.

Another aspect of housetraining that is important to remember is that your dog's ability to "hold" once he realizes he must relieve himself is

also relative to his age. So, when an eight-week-old puppy starts to give cues that he must relieve himself, it's a matter of seconds before he actually is relieving himself. With the very little guys, you will need to be proactive and take him outside sometimes even before he realizes he has "to go."

When he reaches four months of age, from the time he starts cueing that he needs to relieve himself you will have time to get him outside before he has an accident indoors. By eight months of age, he should be able to tell you that he needs to relieve himself and has to go outside.

"Gotta Go" Cues

As noted above, the eight-week-old puppy's timing from cueing that he has to pee or defecate and actually peeing or defecating is so fast that if you see him giving cues to relieve himself, you're almost too late. Keep an eye out for: circling rapidly in place, sniffing with interest, the sudden cessation of play, and for older puppies, running behind a couch, table, or other area in the home that is out of sight.

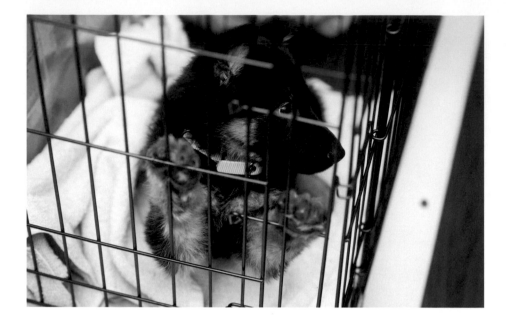

Knowing when your puppy will need to relieve himself is critical in anticipating his needs before he is able to vocalize or show you those needs. Your puppy will need to relieve himself immediately upon waking up (whether it's a nap or an overnight sleep), as soon as he is let out of his crate, within 20 minutes of drinking water, within 10 to 20 minutes of eating a meal, and any time during or after raucous play or exercise. He will also have to relieve himself whenever he becomes very excited (when you come home, for example).

Knowing when your puppy needs to relieve himself will help you in establishing a feeding, exercise, and crating schedule (see "Creating a Routine," page 41).

Making the Crate Comfortable

If used judiciously, a crate can be a GSD owner's best friend when housetraining a young puppy (as well as an older adolescent or an adopted adult dog). For the crate to work as a training tool, the GSD must be happy and content to stay in the crate for increasing amounts of time.

For your GSD puppy's crate, keep in mind that he needs to feel like his crate does not give him enough space to sufficiently get away from his urine or stools, should he have to "go." To create a space that the puppy feels he must keep clean and yet be a space in which the puppy is comfortable, his crate needs to be big enough for your pup to stand up and turn around comfortably and no bigger. Obviously, your puppy is going to grow—and grow a lot in the next several months. So, to keep the puppy's "space" the right size, you can either plan on buying a new crate every time he outgrows his current crate (costly, but if you donate your crates to a shelter, they will be well used and appreciated), or you can purchase an adult-sized crate with a divider and partition off his living quarters, increasing the available living space to the puppy by moving the divider as he grows.

Where you place the crate is also important. It needs to be in an area where the puppy can see what is going on at all times and in a place that is near family. **Note:** this is true for the position of the crate both during the day and at night. If it is too cumbersome to move a full-size crate from the kitchen (day location) to the upstairs bedroom (night position), then consider purchasing two crates.

Once you've got the crate in the correct size and in the correct place(s) in the home, you will need to help your puppy (or adult GSD) associate all good things with his crate. How do you do this? Feed him in his crate. Give him chew items in his crate. Make the crate comfortable for him with soft bedding, such as a sturdy moving blanket or a folded beach towel that is comfortable to lie on but does not contain any filling that he could shred and accidently ingest. Ideally, keep the door to the crate open so the puppy or adult GSD can go in and out at will, unless you can't keep a hawk's eye on him to make sure he isn't giving signs of needing to relieve himself. For little puppies, you can put an exercise pen around his crate to keep him from dashing off into other areas of the home, and for larger pups and adult dogs, you can gate off the room in which the crate is placed to keep him within view at all times. Most importantly, to make your GSD comfortable in his crate, the crate must never be used as punishment, and the total time the GSD is in the crate in a 24-hour period should not be in excess of eight hours.

Does My Crated GSD Need to Relieve Himself?

Both puppies and adult GSDs may cry, whine, or become quite agitated in a crate. Sometimes it is challenging to determine if the GSD simply doesn't want to be in the crate or if he really needs to relieve himself.

If an adult dog is comfortable with crate time and suddenly starts whining, pawing at the crate, or acting restless, he may very well have to relieve himself. A GSD that is acclimating to a crate may become vocal when the door is shut and you walk away. If he has relieved himself completely before being crated, he will be fine in his crate for a short time period. If he does not settle down, his continued alertness in the crate will cause his system to continue to produce urine, effectively filling his bladder sooner than if he were asleep. Active + alert = continued production of urine. Calm + sleep = slower production of urine. So, be aware that adult GSDs that are acclimating to the crate may need to relieve themselves more frequently than GSDs that are completely comfortable in their crates.

An adult dog that is not acclimated to a crate and is *exceptionally* vocal and agitated when left alone in a crate—to the point of self harm—is a different situation. His distress could stem from severe separation anxiety and is a situation that requires professional help from an experienced trainer and/or behaviorist, as well as possible medical intervention from your veterinarian (see, "Separation Anxiety," page 72).

With new puppies, it can be difficult to discern whether the puppy *needs* to relieve himself or if he is crying and whimpering for one of many other possible reasons. When you bring your puppy home, the location is new, the crate is new, the smells are new, *you* are new, and he doesn't have six or more brothers and sisters to pile up with at night. When acclimating a new puppy to his crate, it is helpful to have something with the litter's scent or the mother's scent on it. Some breeders will give you a towel that has been

"scented" with the mother and/or litter to help ease the puppy's transition; others will be willing to "scent" a towel or cloth for you if you bring the breeder a cloth in advance of picking up the puppy.

Without something that has a familiar scent, you could also try placing a towel in his crate that has been sprayed lightly with Dog Appeasing Pheromone (D.A.P.), which is a synthetic copy of the pheromone that a lactating or nursing female dog gives off. All dogs, regardless of age, will recognize this scent and find it comforting. D.A.P. can be found online, in pet stores, and stocked at many veterinary clinics. Other puppy (and rescued adult) owners have found that scenting an article with a small amount of a calming essential oil, such as lavender, or a homeopathic remedy, such as Rescue Remedy, is helpful.

Your GSD puppy may also whine and cry in his crate at night because he is cold. Remember, he's used to sleeping in a warm puppy pile. Set up his crate in an area free of drafts and make sure that he has sufficient bedding to keep him warm.

Your puppy may also be lonely. Not only did the pack of littermates keep him warm, they also kept him company. Now he is alone. For his first couple of nights, it's okay to pull out an air mattress and spend the night next to him. After a couple of nights, however, it is important for your GSD puppy to learn how to self-soothe in the crate. Give him a good chew, such as a Kong that has been stuffed with peanut butter and frozen, as it will serve as something to keep him busy until he falls asleep. Also, you can place a clock that loudly ticks next to the crate to create a steady, soothing white noise, or leave a radio on low volume near his crate.

If in doubt as to why your pup is crying in his crate, it's always better to err on the side of caution and take him outside to relieve himself. A new location, travel, different water, etc., can be upsetting to a puppy's gastrointestinal tract, so he may have a real reason that he wants to get out of his crate.

Creating a Routine

In addition to acclimating your GSD to his crate, you'll want to immediately establish a routine for your dog that will set him up for housetraining success.

The following is a sample schedule for a young puppy.

Wakeup: First thing in the morning, let the puppy out of his crate and immediately take him (carry him and run if you must) to the place outside where you want him to relieve himself. Praise him quietly ("*Good boy*") as he is relieving himself. Bring him back inside.

Breakfast: Once your pup has fully relieved himself, it is time to feed him and provide cool water for him to drink. A young puppy, and even older pups and adult dogs, usually operate on the "food in/poop out" schedule. So, after your pup has finished eating, take him back outside to the "potty place" and allow him to relieve himself. As your pup matures, and as you get a better feel for his bodily functions, you may find that he needs to go out 15 minutes after a meal, or as an older puppy, maybe it's 30 minutes after a meal. Pay attention to what his timing is and how it is changing so you don't wind up standing outside waiting endlessly for him to relieve himself.

Play/training session: After your pup has eaten and relieved himself, now it's time to play, exercise, work on little training sessions, and have fun interacting with him. Make sure to be mindful of time and watch for any cues that your puppy needs to relieve himself again. The more active he is and the more he is drinking water, the more frequently he will need to relieve himself. So, be alert and watchful.

Rest/Naptime: Before putting him in his crate again to rest or to allow yourself to step out of the house, make sure to take him outside to relieve himself one more time in his "potty place." Once he is fully relieved, then you can crate him (shut the door) with a nice chew or something else to safely keep him occupied until he drifts off for a nap. When he wakes up, or anytime you bring him out of his crate during the day, immediately take him outside to his "potty place" to relieve himself.

Dinner: Feed dinner early enough that the pup has time to relieve himself completely before you retire for the evening—6 P.M. or so should be good if you are going to sleep at 10 P.M. or 11 P.M. Follow the cycle from above, taking him out soon after he has eaten, and then watching him

Teach the *Go Potty* Command

Every time your GSD begins to relieve himself, say "*Go potty*" and then praise him. Continue to do this every time he relieves himself. Practice taking the pup out on leash and say "*Go potty*" as he begins to relieve himself, and praise him. When he's off leash, follow him and say "*Go potty*" as he relieves himself and praise him. Soon he will associate the command with relieving himself, or at least trying to. Mixing it up with having the pup on leash sometimes and off leash at other times will also ensure that your GSD is comfortable relieving himself on or off leash. This will help tremendously when you are traveling (and he is on leash). The command will come in handy all the time, particularly when you are rushing to get out the door and your GSD needs to relieve himself *quickly* because you won't be back for a while, or when it is a torrential rain and you don't want to stand outside any longer than you need to.

carefully for signs or cues that he needs to relieve himself and, of course, taking him outside to allow him to do just that.

Bedtime: Before you call it a night, take him out one more time to fully relieve himself. Be aware that he will likely only be able to sleep

Just Say No to Pee Pads

It used to be commonplace for pet owners to "paper train" their puppies. This was accomplished by spreading newspapers over the entire floor of the room where the puppy was residing. In theory, the puppy would learn to relieve himself on the newspapers (easier to clean up than the floor) and as he aged, the puppy owner would gradually reduce the area of the room that had newspapers. When down to the final full spread of newspaper, the puppy owner would take the paper out to the yard to give that area of the yard a scent and the puppy was supposed to learn that the outdoor area was where he needed to relieve himself.

Well, you can imagine how that worked out.

Problem one was that puppies had learned it was okay to pee and poop in the house because that's always where all the newspapers were.

Problem two was that it was quite difficult for most dogs to make the connection that now they were to pee and poop outside.

Problem three was that after paper training a puppy, a newspaper on the floor—or anywhere—was immediate permission to relieve himself on the paper.

Now, fast forward to the invention of pee pads. Pee pads solved the problem of urine absorbing through newspaper and getting on the floor, but it created a new "tactile" problem. In addition to still having to learn to relieve themselves outside when they became too big to use pee pads in the home, puppies had an ingrained tactile experience (paws on a soft, slightly cushy surface) associated with pee pads. This translated into standing on a carpet or rug (similar soft, slightly cushy surface) and thinking all carpets and rugs were good surfaces to relieve themselves on.

Breaking the link that has been made between an ingrained tactile sensation and the act of the pup relieving himself is a very difficult thing to do. (And a reason some dog owners that trained on pee pads converted their floors to all hardwood and/or tile and *no* rugs or carpets, not even an area rug.) So, it's easier to simply not start the association of either peeing and pooping indoors (newspapers and pee pads) or peeing and pooping on carpets, mats, and rugs (pee pads).

a couple hours before he really will need to relieve himself. Do not ignore his request to get out of his crate, as he is in a confined space and you don't want him to have an accident and create a mess. It is just as traumatic for him as it is for you to clean him up in the middle of the night. Additionally, if he relieves himself in such a confined space, you haven't helped to teach him to "hold" when he is in his crate. And, you don't want him to lose his desire to keep his space clean!

Follow this schedule and continue to adjust it with the age and capabilities of your GSD. When he's four months old, he can "hold" for four hours, and you should be able to leave him in his crate during the day for up to four hours, *if* he has been fully exercised, watered, and has relieved himself before you put him in his crate. And, he must be calm in his crate for the time he is in it; otherwise he will need to relieve himself sooner.

When he's six months old, he can "hold" for up to six hours and likely can hold just fine throughout the entire night (i.e., you'll finally get to sleep again). Continue with the schedule and be cognizant of his abilities. Praise good work. If there's an accident, figure out what you may have missed. Did you forget to have him relieve himself right before you put him in the crate? Did you leave him too long in his crate? Did you give him too much access to the house before he was ready? It is usually a good idea not to trust a dog in the home without supervision until he is at least two years old. Until that time, make sure he is crated or has a crate that is open and has access to only one room in the house—preferably the one that is easiest to clean, such as the kitchen.

Special Tips for the Rescued German Shepherd Dog

The good news with an adult, rescued GSD is that he has the *ability* to hold for eight hours during the night and many hours during the day. He also can give you cues that he has to relieve himself with plenty of time to get him outside without having an accident. The bad news . . . he may not be housetrained.

But there's more good news. Training a dog that can "hold" and has the attention/training ability to learn quickly, usually takes far less time than training a young puppy without these physical and mental abilities.

Essentially, to housetrain an adult GSD that is not housetrained, it is necessary to condition him to the crate.

If your rescue GSD is the only dog in the home, you can condition him to the crate by following the puppy instruction earlier in this chapter: Leave the door open to the crate and give the rescue everything good in the crate—treats, food, chews.

If there is already a dog(s) in the house, then gate off a central room (kitchen) for the rescue to acclimate to his crate. Keep his crate in this area with the door open and as before, give him everything good in the crate.

While working to acclimate your new rescue to the crate, keep a close eye on the dog for cues that

he needs to relieve himself. Take him outside every few hours to offer him the opportunity to relieve himself, praise him when he relieves himself, and say quietly the command "*Go potty*" while he is in the act.

Keep a good schedule of taking the rescue dog outside to relieve himself. The same strategies apply: He will need to relieve himself first thing in the morning, as well as within 30 minutes or less of eating a full meal, after play/exercise, and if he has been active or stressed.

Do not allow your adult rescue too much "space" in the house; he will find an area to relieve himself if he has too much area of the house too soon. If you don't want to gate certain areas of your home, you can *tether* your dog to your belt or a belt loop with a long, thinner leash. That way you do not have to give him your full attention but you will know the second he decides to start exploring.

If your rescue is urinating or defecating more than every 3 to 4 hours during the day, there may be an underlying health issue that needs to be checked. Also, a veterinarian appointment would be in order if a previously housetrained dog starts relieving himself in the home—he could have a urinary tract infection (if urinating is the issue) or an intestinal worm or parasite if diarrhea or frequent defecation is the problem.

Additionally, a dog suffering from high levels of anxiety will have a faster metabolism, which in turn will produce urine faster and can be a cause of a dog needing to urinate too frequently (see "Separation Anxiety," page 72 for more tips on preventing and working with the condition).

Chapter Five
The Well-Socialized German Shepherd Dog

The ideal GSD is one that is friendly toward people of every shape and size, as well as dogs of all breeds and mixes. Think how easy this dog would be to take on walks, trips to the park, training classes, hiking, camping, and everyday interactions with people who come to your front door. Sound like a dream? It is a workable goal for every GSD owner.

Genetics Versus Environment

The statement that dog lovers like to make when referring to aggressive dogs, "It's not the dog, it's how you raise him," is not entirely true. Environment (which we'll discuss shortly) is only a factor of the problem. The other factor to consider is the genetic component. Every GSD puppy is born with a predisposition toward a certain type of temperament, and this includes how he will respond and interact with people and dogs. Studies have shown that genetics could impact more than half of a dog's adult temperament and ability to be friendly with other dogs and people. This is why puppy books and articles preach the importance of evaluating the temperament of the parents of the puppy before purchasing the puppy, as temperament does have a genetic component.

With this said, the environment and the experiences that the GSD is exposed to from birth through the first year and a half heavily influence how the genetics come into play for the GSD's temperament. If a GSD that is predisposed to be shy is given proper environmental exposures and positive experiences, he can become a social GSD that is accepting of other dogs and people. Conversely, if a GSD is predisposed to having an outgoing, balanced temperament but experiences a poor environment and negative exposures, he may develop into a fearful adult.

What this boils down to is that you, as the owner of the GSD puppy, are responsible for making the best of your pup's genetic predisposition. Positive experiences will reinforce good behaviors and negative experiences will reinforce undesirable behaviors. Positive experiences will help to create a relaxed GSD that is more comfortable in a variety of situations. One negative experience can be difficult to erase from the GSD's memory, even with multiple, subsequent positive experiences.

But how do you channel the good, positive experiences to develop your GSD into the best dog he can be?

Raising a GSD puppy is an important job and if you are dog-wise and can read a dog's body language, you will be many steps ahead in the puppy-raising game. Knowing dog body language and being dog-behavior savvy will also make your work a lot easier in determining how to help your dog become better socialized with people and other dogs, as well as understanding how to help him overcome feelings of

stress, discomfort, or fear caused by certain places, sounds, movements, etc.

The Importance of Understanding Body Language

"I never saw it coming" and "He bit without any warning" are comments that trainers hear frequently, usually from pet owners in complete disbelief. Let it be known that no dog, in particular the expressive GSD, strikes without giving off body language indicating to everyone and every dog present that he is uncomfortable, stressed, or is growing in agitation. A bite, growl, or charge does not come out of thin air—it's just that many novice dog owners are neither aware of the signs nor know what to do when they see them.

Fortunately, novice handlers can learn to recognize their GSD's body language and what it signifies if they watch and become good "dog listeners." Being a good dog listener and knowing what actions to take when a dog presents certain body language behaviors will significantly help the owner's ability to socialize his or her GSD. It will also help prevent negative experiences during the puppy's most impressionable periods, as the owner can *recognize* the split second a puppy or dog is *about to have* a negative experience. The goal in socialization is to prevent

Be Your Dog's Advocate

It takes time, experience, and keen observance to be able to understand and accurately interpret dog behavior. And although you may be an excellent "dog listener," you must understand that many people in this world *are not* good at interpreting dog behavior. They will rush up on a fearful dog, not know to step away from an agitated dog, and will stick their face right in a dog's face to "accept" kisses.

To help your dog become the most social animal he can become, you must not be afraid to tell others what to do when interacting with your dog. You must step up and be his best advocate as this will help him the most in the long run. And, know that it is *hard* for most of us to be a dog's advocate. It's hard to acknowledge that your GSD is a *dog* and not a little human, and he will behave like a dog.

But, you've got this. Carry on.

negative experiences from happening at all. It is estimated that for one mild negative experience, at least 10 positive experiences are needed to "wipe" away the impact of the negative experience.

When working to socialize a young puppy—or to improve an adult dog's level of sociability—the key is to accrue as many friendly, relaxed experiences as possible for the dog and to avoid all fearful or aggressive behaviors. But, how does a handler avoid negative experiences? By knowing what are considered "green-light" behaviors (friendly, relaxed), "yellow-light" behaviors (the transition behaviors where you have the opportunity, with correct actions, to return your GSD to green-light behaviors), and "red-light" behaviors (those that indicate your GSD is undergoing a negative experience that will now be difficult to "undo").

Behavior Pathways and Physical Expressions: Green-, Yellow-, and Red-Light Behaviors

We all want our GSDs to be in the "green-light" behavior zone. Green-light refers to behaviors that are friendly, relaxed, and calm. Red-light behaviors are not good, and these are the ones that you have perhaps a split second to prevent something really bad from happening to you, another person, or another dog. Yellow-light behaviors are just that: cautionary behaviors. These are the transition behaviors that a dog exhibits when he is deciding if he is going to return to calm, relaxed behavior or elevate into a red-light behavior. It is crucial in socializing your GSD with both people and

son honestly could say they never saw the red-light behavior (bite/attack) coming; however, it would be false for the person to say he or she didn't know the dog was capable of the red-light behavior, as the dog would have shown the transitioning or yellow-light behaviors many times before.

An example of transitioning from green- to yellow- to red-light behaviors is this socialization fiasco: A dog is calm and relaxed while on leash, strolling through a dog-friendly home improvement store when a shopper, who doesn't think dogs should be in the store or is afraid of dogs, sees the GSD and locks eyes with him. If the GSD is shy, the "eye lock" makes him uncomfortable as he interprets the human stare as a threat. Agitated, he moves from friendly, green-light behaviors to yellow-light behaviors of anxiousness and tenseness. The owner in this scenario, instead of recognizing the yellow-light behaviors and turning the dog around in the aisle and heading the other way, continues to walk the increasingly agitated dog *toward the staring human.* At a certain point, the dog is too close to the staring person and his transitioning behaviors turn to red-light, or full-on *fear* behaviors. He either tries to run or he barks aggressively and/or charges the offending human to force the scary human to back away.

Another example is this: You are out on a walk with your GSD. He is on leash and he is calm, relaxed, and showing neutral, green-light

dogs that 1) you clearly recognize a dog's yellow-light behaviors, 2) you know what action to take to return a dog to green-light behaviors, and 3) you never punish a dog for exhibiting a yellow-light behavior, as this is the only opportunity you will have to work on his socialization. If you punish a yellow-light behavior, you will extinguish it—the GSD will no longer exhibit the intermediary or transition behavior and will move directly from a green-light to a red-light behavior. This is exceptionally dangerous and is the one instance in which a per-

behaviors. Then, he spots something of interest. Is it a squirrel? A fast-moving child? Or a little dog? He is now showing yellow-light/transitioning behaviors as he is alert, leaning forward, and determining his next move. Again, if not distracted from the moving object, he could transition into a red-light behavior and set chase to the moving object in the beginning predatory stage, and then possibly into a full predatory stage.

It's scary how quickly things can escalate. However, on a positive note, in the above examples, if the owner had the ability to recognize what was happening, he or she could have taken the correct actions and easily returned the dog to a relaxed state, once again exhibiting green-light behaviors. You as the owner have this power, and you can use it to help your GSD become the best dog he can possibly be. This one fact is empowering to all dog owners, and it is reason in itself to really learn dog behaviors and recognize what you are seeing the second it happens.

Green-Light Behaviors

These behaviors are typically easy to spot and most people can recognize a happy, friendly dog.

Friendly: Ears perked up, eyes wide open, alert look; mouth/teeth are relaxed, possibly slightly open, "smiling" mouth; body has normal posture, still or possibly wiggling of the entire rear end; tail is up or out from body and wagging loosely; vocalization may include soft whim-pering, yapping, or a short, high bark.

Playful/Happy: Ears perked up and forward or relaxed; eyes are wide open, with a happy look to them ("sparkly" or "merry looking"); mouth is relaxed and slightly open and teeth are covered with lips; panting can be from playful excitement.

Curious/Excited: Ears perked up, forward, and pointing toward the object/person/dog of interest; eyes are wide open; mouth is open and teeth are covered by lips, pos-

be to refocus the dog's attention on the handler, and then immediately remove the dog from the situation.

Alert: Ears are perked up, turning to catch sounds; eyes are open normally or are widened; mouth is closed or slightly open but with teeth covered; body is in a normal posture but possibly standing on tiptoe and slightly forward for a somewhat dominant position; tail is up and possibly wagging with stiff and short movements, not in a loose, easygoing wag.

sibly panting; body is with a normal stance, possibly wiggling, standing on tiptoe, or pacing; tail is up and wagging loosely; vocalization can be excited, short barking or whining.

Yellow-Light Behaviors

Yellow-light behaviors are the dog's behaviors or signals that show he is transitioning out of a green-light behavior. Yellow-light behaviors give the handler a warning that something needs to be done *now* to prevent the dog from escalating quickly into a red-light behavior. As noted previously, it is critical that the handler does not punish the dog for exhibiting yellow-light behaviors, as this is the handler's only warning to diffuse the situation. The handler's first reaction should always

Anxious: Ears are partially back; eyes are slightly narrowed; the mouth is closed or slightly open in a "grin"; body is tense and slightly lowered into a submissive position; tail is partially lowered; vocalization is a low whine or moaning-type bark.

Fearful: Ears are laid back, flat, and low on head; eyes are narrowed, averted (avoiding the eyes of a person or dog), possibly rolled back in head, and whites are showing (creating a "moon" eye in which a crescent "moon" forms by the whites of the eyes); mouth has lips drawn back to expose teeth; body is tense, crouched in submissive posi-

tion, shivering, trembling, possible secretion from anal scent glands; tail is down between the dog's legs; vocalization may include low, worried yelp, whine, or growl.

Flight (Beginning Stage): Ears are back against the dog's neck; eyes are wide open, possibly rolled back with whites showing to create a "moon" eye; mouth is slightly opened and drooling is possible; body is tense, shivering, and low as if poised to run; tail is low or between legs; no vocalization or a possible yelp or whine.

Predatory (Beginning Stage): Ears are alert, held forward or backward to catch sounds; eyes are wide open, staring and focused; mouth is closed; body is rigid, low to the ground, ready to spring forward, and the dog is quietly sniffing the air; tail is straight and low; no vocalization (as not to alert the center of attention that they are "prey").

Displacement Behaviors

In addition to green-, yellow-, and red-light behaviors, displacement behaviors are important to recognize and understand. Displacement behaviors are early visual cues that your dog is feeling stressed, anxious, confused, or is trying to suppress an urge to do something else. Displacement behaviors are normal dog behaviors that are displayed out of context and indicate conflict or anxiety.

Displacement behaviors may include:

- Yawning—when he's not tired
- Full body shake—when he's not wet
- Sudden scratching—when he's not itchy
- Lip smacking—when he doesn't have food or isn't anticipating food
- Biting his foot furiously—when he hasn't stepped on anything painful or itchy
- Intense and sudden sniffing the ground or another object—when he wasn't previously interested

Understanding that you are seeing displacement behaviors can be integral in helping your dog have positive experiences, just as when you see yellow-light body language changes.

Chase (Beginning Stage): Ears are perked up, forward pointing; Eyes are wide open and *very* alert; mouth is slightly open and dog is panting excitedly; body is tense, crouched low to a predatory position with legs bent and poised to run; tail is extended straight out from body; no vocalization.

Subordinate/Submissive: Ears are down and flattened against head; eyes are narrowed to slits or wide open with whites showing; lips are pulled way back from teeth in a "grin," nuzzling or licking another animal or person on face; body is lowered to ground with front paw raised or lying on back, belly up; possible urine leaking or dribbling and possible emptying of anal scent glands; tail is down and between the dog's legs; no vocalization or low, worried whining, possible yelping, or whimpering in fear.

Red-Light Behaviors

When the GSD has transitioned into red-light behaviors, the situation is dire, as the GSD is now an immediate threat to those around him. This is the level at which, if action isn't taken within a split second, someone or something is going to be hurt.

Aggressive: Ears are forward or back, close to head; eyes are narrow or staring challengingly; lips are open and drawn back to expose teeth and teeth are bared in a snarl with possible jaw snapping; body is tense, upright with hackles up on neck, and a dominant (on toes, stiff and forward leaning) posturing; tail is straight out from body and hair is extended or "fluffed"; vocalization is a snarl, growl, and/or loud bark.

Guarding: Ears are perked up, and forward; eyes are wide open and alert; mouth is slightly open, teeth are bared and GSD may be snapping or gnashing his teeth; body is tense, rigid, and hackles are up while standing very tall in an aggressive, forward leaning, or dominant stance; tail is rigid, held straight out from body, and sometimes the hairs are extended or "fluffed"; vocalization is a loud alert bark, growl, or snarl.

Dominant: Ears are straight up or forward; eyes are wide open and staring; mouth is closed or slightly open; body is very tall posture and hackles may be up; tail is stiffened and "fluffed," positioned stiffly up or straight out from body; vocalization is low, assertive growl or grunt.

How to Make a Yellow-Light Experience Green

We've spent a lot of time expressing the importance of positive experiences when socializing a GSD with people and dogs. We've also described at length green-, yellow-, and red-light behaviors, as well as how a dog may move between these behavior levels. And, we've discussed how to recognize displacement behaviors. Now that you know what to look for, what do you do to keep your efforts to socialize your GSD positive rather than creating negative experiences that are destructive to his temperament?

1. Watch his behaviors carefully when socializing with people and dogs.
2. Maintain a calm, confident attitude. This is important, as your GSD will pick up on your behaviors. If you are nervous or anxious, he will start to look around to determine what you are worried about. What he picks as the source of your nervousness/anxiety could be completely random and not the actual source—which is usually your nervousness over how he, the GSD, *might* react to something.
3. If he shows a yellow-light behavior, refocus his attention *immediately* on you. You must do this quickly, as your next move is to remove him from the situation. The necessity of refocusing his attention on you first is because if you simply remove him from the situation, the action of remov-

ing him if he is fearful (of the person, place, or thing) is a *reward* for him. This would reinforce his yellow-light, fearful behaviors. Have him refocus on *you and then remove him from the situation*, so that he is being rewarded for his *focus* and not his yellow-light behavior. Use the *"Here!"* command (see *"Here"* on page 95) to regain your GSD's focus quickly.

4. Reward him for his focus.
5. Remove him immediately from the situation.
6. Once he's out of the situation, is comfortable, and has returned to his normal, relaxed behavior, have him *sit* (see *"Sit"* on page 99), praise him, and reward him.

There are also things you *should not* do when your dog moves from being relaxed to a yellow-light behavior (and this includes displacement behaviors, which are a sign of anxiety or a desire to show a more serious behavior):

1. Resist attempting to "comfort" your dog. It's natural to speak to your dog in a higher-pitched voice to try to ease his fears as you would a young child. However, this natural human response to a dog that is stressed or anxious is not appropriate. Here's why: A higher-pitched voice is not soothing to the dog, it is praise. When you praise your dog, you are giving him positive reinforcement— which is exactly what you *don't* want to do if he is fearful, anxious, or stressed.

2. Do not punish your dog for displacement or yellow-light behaviors. As discussed previously, yellow-light behaviors (and displacement behaviors) are your GSD's visible, readable, early warning signs that you can understand. If you punish him when he shows these behaviors, he will stop providing these cues for you. He will still experience anxiety/ stress; however, he will go straight from calm and relaxed to a dangerous, red-light behavior.

Socialization with People

A puppy's initial socialization with people begins with the breeder and his or her family. Good breeders take time to include a lot of human contact with their litters of puppies so that each puppy has received many positive interactions with people of different shapes, sizes, ages, etc. Once you acquire the puppy, it is important that you keep up with his growing socialization skills.

If you have purchased your puppy from a situation in which the puppy has had little human contact, or the interaction he had was less than ideal, it is critically important that you work hard to create as many positive, quality interactions with people as possible. You will not have the advantage that the owner of a puppy from a quality breeder will have, but if you are dedicated (and your puppy has good genetics for a stellar, social dog), you will be able to make up for much of what he is lacking in early socialization skills.

If you are adopting an adult GSD, the kind of socialization experiences he has had are unknown. You will instead be building on his current temperament and socialization skills with people.

Young Puppies (Vaccinations Not Completed)

Little puppies are easy to socialize with people because they are adorable, cute, smallish, and easily transportable virtually everywhere you go. At one time, the recommendation was to create 100 positive interactions with your puppy in his first month with you. This is a possible goal! No one is afraid of a puppy, and 99.99 percent of interactions will be positive as long as you are aware of yellow-light/transitioning behaviors and can easily extricate your puppy from a situation before it becomes a negative experience.

The following are a few tips to set your pup's interactions up for success.

Take him to dog-friendly, non-dog places. Visit places that allow dogs but do not have a lot of dogs present. For example, good places to go would be home improvement stores, feed and tack stores, etc. Avoid any places that have large numbers of dogs present, as the more dogs that walk on a floor or

grassy area, the greater the chance your pup will come in contact with a potentially deadly virus that he's not fully immune to yet (see below). Also, avoid any places in which dogs are off leash, or on leash but poorly controlled. It's important to keep your pup's experiences positive!

Avoid the floor. Since your pup hasn't received all his vaccinations, even locations where only a few dogs are present can create a hazardous exposure situation. To solve this dilemma, put your pup in the shopping cart and wheel him around. Remember to be considerate of other shoppers when using shopping carts in dog-friendly stores. Bring a blanket or towel to put in the bottom of the cart to keep the cart clean and clear of dog hair for the next shopper. Bring sanitizing wipes to thoroughly clean the cart after you're finished using it, too.

Bring treats. As you wheel your pup around, invite friendly strangers to say hello, touch him, pet him, and feed him treats. Make a sincere effort to have your puppy meet and greet a variety of people in a positive, safe environment (where you can control the interaction). Work to introduce him to people of all ages, all races, all genders, people with hats, disabled people, people in motorized wheelchairs, and so on. Be mindful that if he shows any yellow-light behaviors to abort the approach, have the pup focus on you (see pages 55–56), reward him, and then swiftly remove him from the introduction. This is where you must be your puppy's advocate: If he is stressed *do not feel guilty for removing him from the situation*. Yes, we humans feel guilt, shame, even humility when our pups do not act like the stellar, "A-student" of socialization, but as dog owners we must get over this if the end goal is to have a super sociable GSD as an adult. Remember, there is no shame in a dog behaving like a dog; there is,

Rules for Parents with Children
- If you can't supervise, **separate.** This includes leaving your small child in places you think he or she is okay without supervision, such as a swing or rocker, a play pen on the floor, or even a high chair.
- Teach your children the dog rules.
- When supervising, watch your GSD carefully for signs of stress, anxiety, or over-stimulation (as in play) to prevent red-light behaviors from occurring.
- Never allow children to "roughhouse" or "wrestle" with the dog. Ever.
- Train your puppy to be a well-behaved dog and train your children to be respectful children.

however, shame in not being proactive and working to establish a social GSD.

Keep it short and sweet. Always end your socialization adventures on a positive note. Outgoing, happy puppies can and do wear down and become exhausted; leave the store while he is still having a blast. Timid, reserved puppies can become overwhelmed quickly, so if you have one fantastic interaction, celebrate and leave the store on a high note. It is far better to end the socialization session after only a few minutes and after a great interaction than to push

Rules for Children

Note: Children are children and don't always obey the rules; therefore, adult supervision is always essential and it must be both close and 24/7, particularly with children under the age of 10.

- Do not touch the dog if he is sleeping.
- Do not enter the dog's crate *for any reason*.
- Do not try to take away the dog's bone, toy, or food bowl.
- If the dog is in the crate, *leave him alone*.
- If the dog has your toy, do not take it away from him. Get your parent to take the toy back.
- Never hit, poke, or pinch the dog or pull his tail.
- Do not throw anything at the dog.
- Do not hug the dog.
- Do not run in the house or in the yard, unless a parent is with you.

too far or for too long and have a weary or overwhelmed puppy. **Note:** If you accidently work your puppy too hard and he is on the verge of having a poor experience, regain his focus on you (See, *"Here!"* command, page 95), reward him, and then leave the store.

Shy Young Puppies (Not Vaccinated)

It's pretty easy to keep things positive when you are socializing an outgoing, calm GSD puppy. But what if you have a friendly but shy or hesitant puppy? You should still work toward as many positive experiences as possible. Shy puppies should be taken in a shopping cart to stores that allow dogs; however, instead of wheeling him right up to people who want to meet him, keep him at a distance and watch that his behaviors are relaxed. Select people to greet and approach your puppy who appear friendly and dog savvy. Allow only one person at a time to approach your puppy. Tell people

how to approach your puppy to *prevent* him from becoming frightened. (This is where *you* can't be shy and need to be your pup's advocate.)

People approaching a shy GSD pup should keep the approach slow and avoid direct eye contact with the puppy (have them look at his ear or a paw). Treats should be offered with an open palm. If a pup is quite shy, have the person toss him a treat. Pats should be under the chin, as reaching over a puppy to pat him on the top of the head is scary to a shy pup. Remove him from the situation if he becomes uneasy; either wheel him away or literally step in between the person and your puppy, facing your puppy with your back to the person. Stay relaxed and calm. You are in control of the situation. Do not punish him for exhibiting anxious, stressful behaviors as noted previously. These yellow-light behaviors are your guide to how he is feeling. But, do react quickly and calmly when you see he is becoming anxious or stressed, by asking him to *focus* (see "*Here!*", page 95), praise him, and then immediately remove him from the stressor long before he becomes fearful or reactive.

If you feel you simply cannot tell strangers how to approach your dog, then you must become even more creative and create situations in places with people you know. For example, take your pup to a park and have a friend who you've told how to approach your dog and who doesn't mind being coached meet you there. Invite people into your home who you know well and who are willing to help you socialize your pup. Take your pup to your veterinarian's clinic (without letting those paws touch the floor) and have the staff members all say hello to him. These folks know exactly how to approach your pup and how to help you with his socialization. If you are in an area in which your veterinarian feels it's okay to enroll your puppy in an early puppy training class (frequently referred to as "puppy kindergarten"), heed your veterinary professional's advice as to which trainer or school he or she recommends and enroll your puppy. Whatever you do, don't give up on your puppy! You can help him have all positive interactions!

Older, Confident Puppies (Vaccinated)

Now that your pup is fully vaccinated, his paws can touch the floors and you no longer have to worry about coming in contact with communicable canine diseases. Continue socializing him at places that provide contact with many people but do not have many dogs present: home improvement stores, outdoor shopping areas, children's parks (with children), other parks, your veterinarian's office (hello, treats, and leave), outdoor patio style restaurants that allow dogs, outdoor coffee shops, etc.

When introducing your older puppy to people, keep him on a

slack, loose leash. Make sure you've trained him well to *heel* and to *sit* (see Capter 8, Commands Your German Shepherd Dog Needs to Know, pages 95–107). Put him in *sit-stay* to receive pats, treats, and attention. Your pup will realize quickly that sitting gets him attention and will soon start sliding into a *sit* so that he can receive pats and treats. Prevent typical young puppy jumping up behaviors (see "Jumping Up," page 124) in a positive way. You want to encourage confident, happy behaviors and don't want to be in a situation of pulling back hard on a puppy, making him rear up on his hind legs (and putting him in an aggressive lunging position), so that he doesn't jump on someone. Jumping up is a sign of excitement and happiness in young puppies; it's not an aggressive behavior. An older puppy jumping up is obnoxious because he can knock down adults and children. Pulling back so the jumping puppy is now a *lunging* puppy (weight on the forehand and front legs off the ground) puts the puppy in a position (physically) that can lead to aggression (physically and mentally) that the pup learned by being physically shaped into what he recognizes as an aggressive, physical behavior. Teach him a good *sit-stay*. It's much easier!

Shy, Older Puppies (Vaccinated)

Socializing the more hesitant, less confident older puppy is very similar to working with the younger, shy puppy, except now your pup is fully vaccinated and can walk on leash at all the same places he visited before. With the less confident puppy, however, your socialization efforts will focus more on quality over quantity: Your goal is to create opportunities for positive interactions with people and to be less concerned with accruing large numbers of interactions. For the hesitant puppy, every positive interaction will help build his confidence and will make the next interaction easier.

To ensure that his interactions are positive, follow the same instructions for introductions (pages 59–60) as with the shy young pup, always watching for your pup's state of mind, refocusing him first, and then quickly aborting or stepping in-between him and the person if he shows yellow-light behaviors. Praise and reward all good, relaxed, and friendly behaviors.

When you invite people into your home, instruct them to come into the house and ignore the puppy—no direct eye contact, no response or acknowledgment to the puppy's approach, and no patting the puppy. This will allow the puppy to make his own approach to the person. Give the person treats to hold and when the puppy is showing relaxed, green-light behaviors, have the person toss the treat to the puppy. When the puppy is showing calm, relaxed behaviors from a slight distance, the person can offer the pup a treat from his open hand, still not making direct eye contact. Continue until the pup is nudging the person for pats and attention.

With the hesitant pup, you must always be willing to be in charge of the situation and set up your GSD to succeed in his socialization efforts.

Pushy Older Puppies (Vaccinated)

The pushy older puppy is often testing his boundaries with you, as well as with other people he meets. He is one that you will need to pay very close attention to so he maintains positive, green-light interactions with people. Pups usually aren't too pushy until they begin to reach sexual maturity around six months of age. If you have been socializing him from the get-go and he is begin-

ning to show yellow-light behaviors around the six-month point, you will need to make sure your training is successfully refocusing the puppy *immediately* when he displays yellow-light behaviors, and then extricating him from the situation.

If red-light behaviors start appearing as early as four months of age, you may have a serious aggression problem developing that needs immediate attention and a thorough evaluation from a trainer who is skilled in working with behavior issues. Avoid any trainers whose solution is training with an electric shock collar or who uses physically abusive methods. If a dog is truly exhibiting aggressive behaviors, physical methods (such as grabbing the dog by the scruff of his neck, physically trying to throw him on his back in an "Alpha Roll," powerful physical corrections, etc.) will only serve to agitate the dog more and cause heightened and more violent reactions from him.

Socialization with Dogs

The first dog to teach a puppy the do's and don'ts of behaving with other dogs is the puppy's mother. She teaches him that soft play biting is okay but hard biting is not. His littermates teach him that gentle, friendly play is good but over-the-top/dominant play is not. (When littermates play, if they are the vic-

Where *Not* to Take Your Puppy

The greatest risk for your puppy to have a negative experience is at locations that have a multitude of dogs and dog owners in a confined area, indoors or outdoors. Dog parks are particularly notorious for serious and sometimes fatal dog fights, as well as the spread of disease. Other areas, such as popular dog-friendly beaches where people frequently have their dogs off leash (and have no control over them) are also very risky places to take a puppy and are not recommended.

It is sad that the actions of a few dog owners ruin the fun for conscientious dog owners, but it is what it is. Knowing what areas could be problematic and avoiding these places will help to keep your puppy safe and healthy.

tim of a hard bite or bullying, they will cry out and refuse to play with the offending puppy. In this way he learns the beginnings of bite inhibition and that he should respect his elders, as well as appropriate play behaviors.)

Once the puppy leaves the litter, the responsibility of his dog-dog socialization falls on you. Socializing your GSD with dogs is very similar to socializing him with people in that, as the owner, you are setting your puppy up to have positive experiences with other puppies and dogs. You will need to watch for yellow-light or transitioning behaviors. You need to be your dog's advocate and refocus your puppy and remove him from a situation *before* a negative experience happens.

Young Puppies (Vaccinations Not Complete)

Until your puppy has had all his vaccinations (or until your veterinarian gives you the go-ahead to allow your pup to interact with other puppies), set up playtime with vaccinated adult dogs that are kind and gentle. This will continue the dog-dog socialization skills and good dog etiquette that the puppy received from his mom and littermates from birth to eight weeks old. You can also set up playtime with another puppy

that is vaccinated and relative in size to your puppy. A puppy that is too small or too large can be hurt or can hurt the smaller puppy. Keep interactions to a one-to-one basis; larger play groups are not a good idea, even if all dogs are vaccinated, as these groups can get out of hand and spiral into a negative or even traumatic experience for the young puppy.

Older Puppies (Vaccinated)

Continue play sessions with kind, gentle, vaccinated adult dogs and puppies of appropriate size on a one-to-one basis. Add play with a controlled, monitored socialization group of like aged and sized puppies in a training class. (**Note:** It is important that an experienced trainer is present in the socialization

part of a puppy training group. As noted previously, groups of dogs, even puppies, can shift into a negative experience very quickly if someone isn't there to have owners pull out their pups before interactions fall apart.)

Doggie Daycares: A well-monitored doggie daycare group of gentle adults and like-sized puppies could also be an option; however, proceed with great caution. Not all daycare groups are created equally. Some are staffed by people who do not recognize the different warning signs of dogs in the yellow-light range and do not know when to separate dogs. They also frequently do not recognize when a dog is becoming overly excited with play and needs a time out to settle down so he does not break into the yellow or red zones. Additionally, staff members regularly do not recognize when a puppy is getting bullied on the playground, allowing him to experience multiple negative experiences that can shape his entire outlook on other dogs for the remainder of his life.

Play Groups: Breed-specific play groups are sometimes organized by breed rescues, breeders, or like-minded owners in a city or region. If experienced owners are present who can watch for stress, anxiety, displacement behaviors, and yellow-light behaviors—and the group is made up of conscientious dog owners who realize not all dogs enjoy play groups—then this could be a good opportunity for your GSD to play with other dogs. However, most play groups are not run this way, and the GSD often is not a good play group candidate. When GSDs reach sexual maturity, some are not good dog-play candidates because they don't enjoy playing with many dogs. Ultimately, as long as your adult GSD is tolerant (non-aggressive/non-fearful) of other dogs, you have reached your goal.

Socializing the Rescued German Shepherd Dog

Rescued GSDs come with a history. Some have a good history with socialization. Many more have not had appropriate socialization. Reputable GSD rescues do not place dogs that have poor people skills with families. In addition, shelters with fostering services, animal behaviorists, and skill trainers on staff or serving as volunteers, can fully analyze a dog's social skills.

With dogs from these sources, listen to the rescuers' advice, follow it closely, and begin training your GSD immediately. (Ask the shelter or the rescuer who they recommend. They will be a valuable resource for training and behavior consultations.)

Socializing the Rescued GSD with People

When it comes to socializing with people, you will want to build on what the shelter, rescue, or breed rescue has started. Work on obedience skills (*heel, sit, sit-stay,* and *down*) so that you can begin taking your dog to areas with people and continue to socialize him. Good areas to visit are those with people but not packed with people. Early morning visits to parks, home improvement stores, garden centers that allow dogs, etc. are usually best, as these places are not nearly as busy at this time.

Work with a reward system. Figure out the reward that he loves the best—it could be food, a ball, or a tug—and make sure you reward him when he is showing calm, relaxed behavior. Allow selected people to offer him a treat when he sits. Do not be anxious or stressed yourself but do be very aware of body language and yellow-light behaviors (see pages 52–54).

Until you know precisely how friendly your GSD is with people, follow the "shy puppy" guidelines for introductions on pages 59–60. Never put yourself or anyone else in danger—in other words, if your GSD can't go anywhere without displaying yellow-light behaviors or displacement behaviors or it is difficult for you to control him on leash, consult a trainer immediately. Understand that the need to work with a trainer is not a reflection of your abilities as an owner or the potential sociability of the dog; it *is* a reflection of your earnestness in accomplishing your goals of having a controllable, sociable GSD that is pleasant to take on walks and can be trusted around people.

Socializing the Rescued GSD with Dogs

When it comes to socializing your rescued GSD with other dogs, your goal is not to create a fantastic dog-run play buddy—as many GSDs as adults are generally not suitable for big dog parks and don't enjoy it as much as other breeds seem to. Rather, your goal is to help your GSD be calm and relaxed around other dogs.

One of the best ways to help your dog adjust to being around other dogs while maintaining green-light behaviors is to walk him with another dog and handler. Make sure the other dog is gentle and tolerant. This exercise *does* require that your dog is controllable on leash, is able to focus on you, and *heel*. If he is not reliable on leash, wait to work on

his socialization with dogs until he is reliable.

At first, have the dog and handler walk in front of you and your GSD. Keep your dog at a distance, at which he is showing no transitional/yellow-light behaviors. Walk until he is relaxed and you can move closer to the dog in front. Reward good behavior with praise and occasional treats. If at any time he becomes uncomfortable, increase his distance from the dog until your GSD is relaxed again. Continue to work to get closer to the dog in front of you without your GSD showing any signs of yellow-light/transition behaviors. Reward only good behavior.

When he is comfortable walking about a dog's length behind the other dog, move up to a position in which you and the other handler are walking side-by-side with the dogs on the *outside* (people in the middle). Your goal here is to achieve a calm, relaxed walking dog.

Next, walk side-by-side with the dogs in between the handlers but at a distance apart that is comfortable for your GSD. Your goal continues to be to have your GSD calm and relaxed while walking, and exhibiting no transitional behaviors. If he can't do this, put the dogs back on the outside of both handlers again. Keep working until the dogs can walk side-by-side without issues.

Only when the dogs can walk side-by-side without any issues is it okay to allow the dogs to check each other out while on leash. Make

the "check out" brief and continue walking. Separate the dogs immediately (and calmly) if any transitional behaviors begin to show. If the first greeting went smoothly, stop for another one and continue walking.

The next time you walk with the same dog, do not immediately go to the side-by-side walking; rather, begin with the other dog in front and yours in back, and work back up to the side-by-side walking.

The process takes patience, but every time you're able to accomplish a positive experience walking in the near proximity of another dog, you have gained a step toward your GSD's socialization skills.

Note: Avoid putting your GSD in a position in which an off-leash dog is allowed to run up to him while he is on leash. Regardless of how "friendly" the other dog is purported to be (it's a guarantee that the owner will holler "Don't worry! He's friendly!" when you can clearly see the offending loose dog is showing yellow- or even red-light behaviors),

an off-leash dog running toward an on-leash dog is offensive and frightening to the leashed dog. Public beaches and large dog-friendly parks are two areas where dogs are frequently allowed to run off leash and are places to be avoided or approached with alertness and extreme caution (i.e., go to these places at times of day when there are few dogs present, if any).

Chapter Six
Habituation

Habituation is the process of acclimating your GSD to everyday sights, sounds, and movements at and around the home. Your breeder started your GSD's habituation by having the pups whelped and nursed in the home. Puppies learn from their mother's reaction to everyday sights and sounds and movements in the home. If the puppies' mom doesn't react to a toilet flushing, the puppies won't either.

Being raised in the home, the puppies are exposed to ceiling fans spinning, toasters popping up toast, doors opening and shutting, and people coming and going, as well as plates rattling and water sloshing in a dishwasher, garage doors opening, microwaves beeping, etc.

Again, if the puppies' mom doesn't react, then the puppies learn not to react. If your puppy was not raised in the home or if you have a rescue that wasn't home raised, then everything they see, hear, and feel is new to them.

In effect, once the pup or rescue comes to your home, you become the GSD's role model for reactions to sights and sounds in the home. How you react (or don't react) will impress on the GSD how he should respond.

Handling Home Introductions with the GSD Puppy

Ignore any *negative* reactions your pup may have to anything in the home. If he *does* react (startles, slinks, barks, etc.) to a sight, sound, or movement, do not direct any attention toward the puppy, and maintain a confident attitude while going about your business. He is looking to you to learn how to react to the new sight, sound, or movement. When he no longer reacts negatively to the sight, sound, or movement, you can praise him. Remember not to punish him for showing anxiety, stress, or a yellow-light behavior to a sight, sound, smell, or movement in the home; this will remove the warning behavior and it has the potential to make his reaction stronger to the same sight, sound, or movement the next time he is exposed to it.

Be careful how you react to a yellow-light situation with habituation, too; problems can ensue if you try to ease a dog's reaction to something with physical or verbal "comfort." Humans tend to use high-pitched voices to reassure a dog that something is okay. This is not okay because the dog interprets a high-pitched voice as praise. So, your GSD does not know the difference between "It's okay, little guy" and "Good boy"—they are both positive reinforcements that he has done something right as he tunes into the tone and pitch of the voice. Therefore, inadvertently praising an adverse or unwanted reaction to a sound in the home *reinforces* the behavior and makes the problem *worse.* He is being rewarded and encouraged to continue to react to stimuli and to react more strongly the next time he sees, hears, or feels them.

Give Your GSD a Safe Observation Place

Acclimating your GSD to his crate (see "Crate Training," pages 35–45) is helpful not only in house-training but also in familiarizing your GSD—whether a puppy or an adult—to the sights and sounds of your home. If he associates all good things with his crate (i.e., snacks, treats, meals, chewy bones, sleeping, resting, etc.), the crate then becomes a safe observation location for him to see and hear new sights and sounds without feeling like he is in danger.

Place is another way to create a safe place for your GSD to observe daily sights and sounds. *Place* is often a blanket on the floor that a puppy or dog is taught to go to and relax. This is helpful in the home because it gives the GSD another place to go that he associates with relaxing and being calm. It also allows you to take a "place" from a specific spot in the home to other areas in the home and when traveling. Putting "place" on the end of the bed in a hotel room indicates to the GSD where he is to go to relax.

Training *Place*

Step 1: Select a blanket or light pad that you can move to various places easily. Put the blanket on the floor.

Step 2: Get your dog's attention, and lure him (see "Lures," page 86) over to the blanket.

Step 3: As soon as his paws are on the blanket, say, *"Place!"*

Step 4: Praise him

Step 5: Release him with an *"OK!"* so he can move off the blanket.

Step 6: Reward him.

Step 7: Repeat and practice.

Step 8: Make the exercise more difficult, incrementally. When your GSD has made the association of *"Place!"* with the blanket, begin saying *"Place!"* when he is a step away from the blanket. Release, reward, and repeat. Then, back up the command so that you give it when he is a couple of steps away. Release, reward, and repeat. Keep working so that you can say *"Place!"* and your GSD is running to find his "place" and standing on it.

Step 9: Add a *sit* to finish the *place* command. Starting near the blanket, tell him *"Place!"* and when he gets all four paws on the blanket, ask him to *"Sit."* (See *"Sit!"* on page 99.) When he sits, release, reward, and repeat. Continue to work on the exercise, making it incrementally harder (increase distance from the blanket) until he has fully linked finding the blanket *and* sitting with the *place* command.

Step 10: Add the *down* command. Start with the blanket nearby; tell him *"Place!"* He should go directly to the blanket and *sit.* (If he doesn't, go back to linking the *sit* as the final action of *place.*) Give

him the *down* command. When he is fully in a *down*, release with an "OK!" Reward and repeat.

Step 11: When you have *place* at the point where you can give the command, and your GSD runs to the blanket and lies down, make it harder by adding the *stay* (see "Stay" on page 100) to the end of the *place* command.

The exercise may sound long and tedious but it's not. With this type of exercise—that is teaching a series of behaviors and linking them together—it is important to break it down into small steps. In this way, your GSD has the greatest opportunity to understand what he is being taught and to learn it as quickly as possible. Your ultimate goal is to tell your GSD to *"Place!"* and he will seek out his blanket, lie down, and relax.

Preventing Separation Anxiety (SA)

Acclimating and habituating your GSD to the home is important but don't forget—it is equally important to habituate your GSD to being alone. He must be able to relax in his crate and accept that this is okay and that you will come back.

GSDs are a bit more prone to suffer from separation anxiety than other breeds. The level of a dog's SA can vary from mild whining when you leave to full-blown catastrophe the second you pick up your house keys (i.e., destruction of bedding in crate, urinating in crate, defecating, frantic clawing and gnashing of teeth that bloody paws and break teeth, etc.).

Preventing SA from developing is much easier than trying to cure a dog suffering from SA, which involves much patience and time.

When working with a puppy, you are undoubtedly making every effort to socialize him, so you are taking him with you everywhere. This is excellent, but he has to be left at home alone regularly, too, to prevent him from developing SA when he is older and possibly you aren't taking him out as much.

First, make sure he is acclimated to the crate so he feels it is a safe environment. Give him a good chew that will take some time to work on (sort of like a pacifier). When you leave the house, be confident and

Choosing a Crate for the SA Dog

Open wire crates allow a dog to have a 360-degree view. The wire crate is also cooler in the summer and can be covered with a heavy blanket in colder weather or if the dog likes a den-like feel. The cons to a wire crate are that the structure allows serious SA dogs to grab wires and possibly break teeth and pull or break nails. Panicked dogs can pull covering (or any fabric close to the crate) into the crate and destroy it.

A plastic crate is less likely to cause a panicked dog to break teeth or catch nails, and it is easier to clean up than a wire crate if the GSD soils it. A con is that some dogs feel closed in, and if so, this style crate could increase stress levels. Another con is that the airflow in a plastic crate is not as good as in a wire crate.

You can determine what crate is best for your SA dog when you know what causes him the most stress and how likely he is to harm himself.

very matter-of-fact. Do not make a ritual out of leaving (i.e., checking door locks, putting purse in a specific location, grabbing keys, double checking door locks, etc.) because your puppy will learn your rituals and will know you are leaving long before you leave. Grab your keys and go. Come back. Let the pup out of his crate and take him outside to relieve himself. Repeat. Leave the house even if you don't have anywhere to go, just so that you can teach your puppy that you will leave and you will come back and nothing bad will happen.

Treating Separation Anxiety

If you have adopted an adult dog or are working with an older puppy that has developed separation anxiety, how you proceed will depend on how severe the separation anxiety is. **Note:** In severe cases—in which the dog injures himself in the crate and is a danger to himself if left alone—veterinary medical intervention may be required to help calm the dog to a point where he won't injure himself as you work on conditioning him to your leaving.

For lesser, but still stressful, cases of separation anxiety, work on the following:

Condition your GSD to the crate as a safe, secure place (see pages 38–39). Next, work to desensitize him to "departure" cues.

Departure cues are all those trivial things that you do in preparation to leave the house. They could involve locking doors, shutting windows, picking up car keys, grabbing a jacket, putting on your shoes, etc. A dog suffering from SA will know the subtleties of your routine up to an hour before you leave the home.

To desensitize him to your departure cues, you will have to provide these cues out of context—or not in conjunction with leaving the house.

When your GSD is not in the crate or he is relaxing in the crate with the door open, pick up your keys and put them back down. Open the front door and shut it. Lock the back door and unlock the back door. Put on a jacket, walk around for a while, and take off the jacket. Pick up your wallet or purse, carry it around, and put it back down. Continue to do anything you can think of that you typically do up to an hour before leaving the house, but don't leave the house.

Then, add a layer of departure cues. Put your GSD in his crate, give him a good chew, close the crate door, pick up your keys and put them back down. Open the front door and shut it. Lock the back door and unlock the back door. Put on your jacket, walk around for a while, and take off jacket. Pick up your wallet or purse, carry it around, and put it back down. You get the idea. Then, let him out of his crate. You are continuing to desensitize him to all the cues you give prior to leaving. The hope of desensitization exposures is that with enough time and practice, the "departure" cues are no longer signs that you are leaving.

Training *I'll Be Back*

The purpose of this command is to condition your dog to understand that he is waiting in place until you come back.

Step 1: Put him in his crate, and say "*I'll be back*" in a normal *voice.* A high-pitched voice is praise and will confirm to him that he needs to be distressed because you're leaving.

Step 2: Walk away, and then come back.

Step 3: Praise him *if* he is calm, and release him from his crate.

Step 4: Repeat and extend the time that you walk away and come back, and always stay in his sight.

Step 5: Mix this exercise up with the previous exercise of performing departure cues and not leaving.

Step 6: Increase the difficulty of the crate exercise by putting him in the crate, saying, "*I'll be back*," then walk out of his sight and come right back; walk to the door and come right back; walk to the door, open and shut it, and come right back; walk to the car, open and close the door to the car, and come right back; walk to the car, get in and start the engine, turn off the engine, and come right back, etc.

Step 7: Continue to include the "*I'll be back*" exercise with the desensitization to departure cues exercise. Remember, this will take time—typically many weeks or even months of work for a seriously distressed SA dog.

Exercise and Mental Stimulation Helps

Make it part of your GSD's daily routine to exercise him, and exercise him well—not to the point of exhaustion, but to the point where, when you put him in his crate, he is tired and ready to settle down for a nap. Additionally, make sure your anxious GSD is receiving enough mental stimulation with plenty of training, as well as time with interactive toys that require thinking to receive a treat. If your GSD is physically and mentally stimulated, then the question "Is it lack of exercise and/or mental stimulation, or is it really SA?" will be removed from the equation.

Helping your GSD overcome SA takes time, patience, and practice. If you do not work out of the home and must leave for extended periods of time, make alternate plans for your severely distraught GSD. Continue (while you are at home) working on the desensitization exercises, but when you leave enlist a trusted friend that the dog likes to stay with your GSD when you leave the house. If he is perfectly content to stay at home with a human friend, his real problem may be isolation disorder. If this is the case, his anxiety stems from being left alone and if a human—any human—is with him, he is fine.

If you can't have a friend stay with your GSD for several minutes before

Is It Really SA?

GSDs do not like to be left alone; it is their nature to want to be with you 24/7. And, just like very intelligent human children, they do know how to express themselves about their feelings of being left behind. Often, owners are surprised at how their supposed SA dogs behave when they are gone.

Curious? Purchase a baby monitor that has audio and even video, and see what your dog does when you leave him after 5, 10, and 20 minutes. Does he settle down completely and then suddenly pick up on the whining, barking, panting, drooling, and teeth gnashing when he hears you approaching the front door? Then he doesn't have SA, and he probably just needs something to do while you're gone, and for you to have a calm, confident, you'll-be-fine attitude when you leave.

If, on the other hand, your GSD continues to whine, cry, bark, pace, pant, claw, and show other signs of stress and anxiety for the duration of your time away from the home, then you do have a dog with SA, and can help lessen his stress and anxiety using the steps described on pages 73–75.

you leave, and for 30-minutes or more after you leave, consider taking your dog to a trusted trainer/doggie day care where he can be occupied and have fun while you are gone. Continue to work on desensitizing him to your departure cues.

With any level of SA, it is always wise to seek professional veterinary and behaviorist assistance. Some medications available from your veterinarian can help calm your GSD while you are training him through desensitization methods. Some nonprescription nutritional supplements or homeopathic remedies may also be helpful for your dog, such as Rescue Remedy, DAP plug-ins, and sprays. Also, check with your veterinarian for recommendations, as new products may have become available on the market, and/or recent studies may indicate that certain nutraceuticals may be effective in lessening dogs' stress reactions. For more

information on SA and how to desensitize your dog to departure cues, consider this older but still good resource: *I'll Be Home Soon: How to Prevent and Treat Separation Anxiety*, by Patricia B. McConnell, Ph.D.

Thunderstorms

Some GSDs are often sensitive to thunderstorms. And unfortunately, thunderstorms are not predictable enough for desensitization techniques to work.

Symptoms of thunderstorm anxiety include pacing, drooling, panting, shaking, whining, barking, clawing, and digging. A GSD can have such an extreme case of thunderstorm anxiety that it can be classified as a panic disorder with an intense flight response.

Desensitization methods (playing sounds of thunderstorms, thunderstorms mixed with classical music, etc.) have not been shown to work clinically. It is thought that the trigger for the extreme thunderstorm reaction is more than the ear-splitting sound; rather, it is a combination of electrical sensations, weather pressure changes, and the vibrations of thunder when it shakes the house, etc., all of which cannot be replicated to desensitize a dog.

Previous medicinal treatment recommendations included Xanax or other human antianxiety meds, but these had limited success. Sedatives were sometimes used, too, but they

usually created an anxious, sedated dog, which even worsened the dog's thunder anxiety.

Current veterinary treatments include norepinephrine that is dosed via a gel in-between the dog's gums and cheek. This form of the drug was introduced in 2016 and has shown moderate success in some dogs for noise aversion, too.

Various wraps and shirts have been designed for dogs with thunderstorm anxieties, and these have a mixed result in effectiveness. The shirts and wraps are meant to mimic the pressure of a hug; however, some dogs do not like this feeling.

Holistic treatments are available for thunderstorm phobias, such as homeopathic oils, which can be rubbed on the dog's gums, as well as calming essential oils that can be worn in an amulet on the dog's collar. The dog's blanket in his crate can be given a light spritz of DAP, a calming, synthetic pheromone.

Noise Aversion

It is reported that one quarter to one third of all dogs have some level of noise aversion. July 5 is the biggest day for stray pickups in the U.S.; New Year's Day is a close second. One positive, however, is that unlike thunderstorm anxiety, noise aversion is a condition that you can work with, as it is much more predictable than a storm. For example, for the most part you know when fireworks are going to occur.

On nights that there is an elevated risk of fireworks, with a noise-averse GSD, make sure the dog is safely contained indoors, and ensure that he is wearing a form of easy identification. Although he may never have scaled your backyard fence or tried to dig out, his panic level may become so great that he will do anything to escape. Once he gets out, he may run for miles and miles. If you need to take him outside to relieve himself, walk him on leash and with a collar that he can't back out of or escape from (such as a martingale collar that tightens when he pulls but is wide enough that it is not a choke collar). Consider using holistic remedies *before* the fireworks begin, such as DAP, Rescue Remedy, or Essential oils in an amulet. Additionally, talk to your veterinarian about Sileo, a treatment that has seen some success treating noise aversion, as well as thunderstorms.

During hunting season when gun shots are sporadic, follow the same guidelines as for fireworks, and consider using a holistic treatment that can be used every day or worn as an amulet.

Light Chasing

You've seen the videos of cats chasing the light cast from a pen light. The videos look fun; however, do not start this pen light chasing game with your GSD. There is a real condition that occurs with GSDs that involves the overstimulation of the GSD to lights or to the shadows created by strong lights. When overstimulated, the dog will attack not only the track of the pen light, but *any* flashes of light. Unlike that cat that just pounces on the light beam, the GSD will tear up wherever the flash of light strikes. He may also extend this to attacking shadows. The danger here is that play quickly escalates from overstimulation to light, flashes of light, and/or shadows to red-light behaviors, including full-on aggression.

If you've already made the mistake of playing with a pen light and your GSD now has this overstimulation to light, flashes, and/or shadows, seek professional help—this can be a very difficult behavior to change.

Car Travel

To take your GSD with you everywhere, you will want him to be acclimated to car travel. A drooling, panting, restless full-grown GSD is no fun in the car, so begin this life skill early.

When your GSD is an adult and used to car travel, you can choose to safely harness him into the back seat or use a car divider in the back of an SUV to make the entire back end of the truck a comfortable, if oversized, crate. Until that time, it is wise to use a crate for puppy car travel. The crate is his safe spot, so he will recognize it as a safe spot in the car. If he does have an accident or gets sick, it's far easier to clean a crate than to clean your upholstery.

When traveling by car, make sure the pup's crate is well ventilated and that he is as cool in his crate in the back seat as you are in the front seat. If your pup is traveling in a solid plastic crate, consider attaching a separate, battery-powered fan to the outside of his crate so that he can remain cool. Also, make sure he has access to cool water. Crate bowls attach to the metal mesh of the crate

Car Harnesses

Once your GSD has matured and travels without stress in the car, you can either continue transporting him in a crate, or you can look at a seat belt buckle/harness system. The harness for this system generally has padding and a sturdy loop and buckle that are designed to allow your GSD to stand up, turn around, and lie down, but not go any farther than that. It will protect your GSD from becoming a flying projectile in your car should you stop abruptly. To make the transition from crate to harness system, condition your GSD to the harness. Allow him to wear it around the house and reward him for good behavior. It will not take him long to associate the harness with a car ride. And, because car travel is associated with all things good for a dog, he will be happy when he sees you bring his harness out.

door so the pup can't tip and spill his water. To ensure that he doesn't create a soggy mess in his crate, put ice cubes in his bowl. Give him a favorite chew in the crate to keep him occupied while traveling.

Associate car travel with really fun things. If the only time you take your GSD in the car is to take him to the veterinary clinic for his vaccinations, he will not associate car rides with fun times. So, take short trips to local parks for a quick walk. Go to a hardware store that allows dogs. Take him to go pick up the kids from school. Visit an outdoor shopping mall. You don't have to go far, just go somewhere fun. Bring treats with you so that you can continue your GSD's socialization and work on little train-

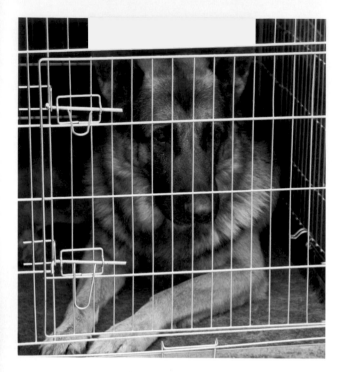

ing exercises. Take a few of his favorite toys to play fetch on a long leash, if you're not in a safely fenced area. And, make trips to the veterinarian as social calls. Most veterinarians and their staffs love a non-appointment visit from their clients, and they come stocked with their own healthy treats, too! Making these extra trips to the veterinary office also helps to lower your GSD's anxiety when he has to go to the veterinarian because of a health issue.

Travel Anxiety Some dogs are never bothered with car travel and act as if they've been doing it all their lives. Most GSDs will need some conditioning to car travel but acclimate well over time. Anxiety and stress symptoms may include panting, drooling excessively, whining,

Never Leave a Dog Unattended

Cars heat up exceedingly quickly when the windows are shut. Countless dogs have died after being shut in a car while owners run into a store "for a few seconds." It's a horrible way to die and completely preventable.

Even rolling down the windows in a car can be dangerous. If your dog is not secured, he could jump out and try to follow you. If he is secured, someone may try to reach in to pet him and get bitten—it is *his* car you've left him to guard. Additionally, he could be stolen. And finally, he could still get over-

heated easily, even with the car windows open and the car parked in the shade. He has no way to cool himself.

Leaving the car locked and running with the air conditioning blowing is *better* but it is still not fail-proof. Air-conditioning units can fail and then your dog is in a locked car with no ventilation.

Bottom line, if the weather is above 70 degrees, when you stop the car, your dog goes with you. If he can't, make sure someone sits with him in the air-conditioned car so that if something fails, your dog can be moved to a shady location outside of the car.

barking, shaking, vomiting, defecating/urinating. If your GSD has more than a slight case of travel anxiety, there are techniques that can be used to help him adjust to the car.

Car Sickness It is not uncommon for puppies to have issues with travel sickness. Puppies can be a little anxious in the car, but more often their car sickness is an equilibrium issue in the inner ear that typically resolves with age. If your puppy's car sickness does not resolve by 12 months of age, or he continues to be overly anxious in the car, consult with your veterinarian. Medications are available for car sickness. Some medications that work with the anxiety issue are used for calming purposes, and lessen stress and

potentially non-physical reasons for vomiting. Other medications are for nausea, and treat the physical reasons for vomiting. The anti-nausea medications that are now available are non-drowsy, so your dog is ready to play whenever you reach your location; however, they must be given two hours prior to departure. These medications may also lessen a dog's anxiety with future car travel, as the GSD is able to travel comfortably and relax without vomiting.

Conditioning for Car Travel

With any acclimation efforts, baby steps are key in making an anxious GSD enjoy car travel. If you have a particularly anxious GSD, follow these steps.

Acclimate your GSD to his crate. If he's comfortable in his crate in the home, now you need to acclimate him to the crate *in the car*. Start by feeding him in the car in the crate. Do not drive the car—do not even start the car. If it is warm outside, make sure the car is parked in the shade and all the doors and windows are open. Give him treats in the car in the crate. If all is going well, put him in the crate with a favorite treat, and turn on the engine. Reward/praise him if he shows no signs of anxiety.

Next, put him in the crate, turn on the engine, back down the driveway, return. Yes, your neighbors will think you're nuts but that's okay. Repeat these steps over a period of days until the GSD is comfortable. Reward and praise him when he shows no anxiety.

Keep increasing his exposure to the crate, the car, and travel. Put him in the crate, turn on the engine, and drive around the block. Continue to lengthen the time of the drive. Visit a location during the drive that is fun. Get out and play, walk around. Continue to condition your GSD to car travel and work on associating fun places and activities with the car ride.

When is it time to work with a veterinarian? If the puppy is 12 months old and still gets sick in the car (see "Car Sickness," page 81), or if your GSD was previously fine traveling in a car and is now suddenly anxious or nauseous, consult your veterinarian.

Home Habituation for Rescued Adult Dogs

Rescued dogs are more likely to react to lights, noise, sounds, and movements of everyday home life and travel. Some rescues have either not been raised in a home or possibly had a negligent or even an abusive home.

So, it is not uncommon for a rescued adult GSD to be startled or display an anxious response to a stimulus in the home. What you do when your GSD reacts to a sound, for example, will help him react less the next time he hears it. So, what do you do? Nothing. Don't react. Think about when the GSD was a puppy and he was acclimating to the sights, sounds, and movements at his breeder's home. He learned how to respond to things from his canine mother. If she spooked or jumped at a sound, he learned to be startled or to be afraid of a sound. If she didn't react to a door slamming, he learned not to react to a door slamming. So, in effect, you are providing the leadership figure to help him determine if something is a valid reason to be alarmed or if it's "nothing."

So, let's say your toast pops up in the toaster and your GSD panics in fear on the floor. Do nothing. Remain calm and confident and act like the GSD never reacted. When the dog picks himself off the floor, and regains a calm demeanor, then you can tell him he's a good dog.

To acclimate him to the sound (because you now know the pop of the toaster makes him jump), toast an extra piece of bread now and again. Don't expose him to the sight, sound, or movement to the point of overwhelming him, but don't stop toasting your bread *because* he is frightened. Also, remember not to reassure him if he is frightened by something. Speaking in a high voice in an attempt to comfort a dog is teaching the wrong thing; you are praising him for reacting, and he will continue to react more strongly each time. Also, remember not to punish him for showing his anxiety or fear. Punishing yellow-light behaviors will teach him to drop the yellow-light behavior and go straight to a red-light behavior—and now you have created an enormous problem.

Aggressive responses to a stimulus in the home require professional help. Aggression is a red-light behavior, and the reason behind why he responds in such a manner does not matter. This is not a response to a stimulus that can be treated safely through a desensitization program. For example, let's say you pick up a broom to sweep the porch and the rescued GSD comes flying over and aggressively attacks the broom. The reason does not matter at this point because if you attempt to condition him to the broom through exposures, it will not desensitize the dog; rather, it will increase his aggressive response and you could be caught in the middle. Contact a professional trainer or behaviorist for help.

Chapter Seven

Beginning Command Training

Training Tools

Dog training begins with a dog and a handler. Success includes a good attitude, patience, and consistency. And the only supplies needed are a simple collar and leash and a few treats as reinforcements for reward-based training.

What Collar to Use?

What you want to purchase for a puppy is a flat, buckle collar—or a quick-release collar. Both of these collars are adjustable, so they can be made larger as your pup grows. The collars only adjust so much, however, so you will need to purchase at least two to three collars in your pup's first 18 months. A properly fitting collar will allow you to comfortably put two fingers in between the collar and the dog's neck. You don't want the collar so loose that if the GSD starts to back up, it will pop off his head.

Flat, buckle collars and quick-release collars are appropriate for training because they don't apply pressure on the neck. Harsh methods, like training/choke collars, are never necessary and should not be used. Puppies that begin training at a young age can be worked with a buckle collar throughout their lives. If you are working with an older puppy or a rescued adult, a combination of a buckle collar and a head collar (a halter-type tool that when the dog pulls, he turns around to face you, eliminating the effectiveness of pulling) can be combined to give you more control when walking.

In extreme cases with very heavy pullers, your trainer may advise the non-aggressive use of a prong collar. The prong collar is never to be tugged, pulled, popped, or otherwise used on anything but a slack leash *ever*. This collar works by tightening when the dog pulls against the leash. The prong collar is only recommended for use under the careful guidance of a trainer.

And, finally, under no terms should an electric collar be used to "control" a GSD. Aggression and abuse by the handler will beget aggression in return from the dog, or result in a GSD that will completely shut down.

Leash

Leashes come in a variety of lengths and materials. A good length for training is six feet. This will give you enough length that you can work on *sit-stay, down-stay,* and *come* with a little bit of distance. As for the material, nylon is very durable, but woven cotton is a bit more comfortable to hold. Leather is nice on hands, but it is a bit pricier and

puppies (and adult GSDs) love to chew on leather, making it a bit more expensive to replace when—not if—your puppy chews on it.

Make sure to pay attention to the size of the leash's clip when purchasing a leash for a small puppy. There's nothing worse for a puppy than getting clobbered in the head repeatedly by a heavy, brass clip when he is trying to do his best. You'll need to buy more than one leash in the GSD's lifetime; so, for the little puppy, purchase a leash with a small clip. It's not a great expense, and you can donate the puppy leash to a shelter.

Lures: What to Use

Typically, the "lure" that is used to shape a dog's behavior is a small treat. It can also be a ball or a ball on a rope, as GSDs are often more apt to work for a ball than they are for a treat. Regardless of what you use to shape your dog's behavior, the lure should be the same thing you use to reinforce the behavior (see "Reinforcements," page 88).

Ways of Learning a New Behavior

There are several ways in which a dog can learn a new behavior. One of the most common methods used in positive, reward-based training is the use of a lure—a high-value treat or toy—to shape the dog's behavior.

Luring One of the greatest advantages to shaping a behavior with a

Physical Manipulation

Physically positioning a dog into a *sit* or a *down* was common practice decades ago and was usually the method employed in puppy training classes where the puppies were small and still fairly malleable. In other words, the puppies would allow their owners to push and pull their legs and bodies to position them into a *sit* or a *down*. With small puppies and adult dogs that were not apt to challenge their owners ever, this method worked okay. Physical manipulation does not work with a confused, strong adolescent dog or a full-grown adult dog. Additionally, this method can be dangerous when used with a reactive dog that feels he is in command of the relationship.

lure is that a handler of any size can confidently shape the behavior of a full-grown dog without ever touching the dog. This is very important when working with unknown adult dogs that may not be used to physical handling—even in a positive way—and strong adolescent and adult dogs that see physical positioning as a confrontation. Using a lure is a really easy method to achieve the desired behavior in a non-confrontational way.

Learning by association Dogs frequently learn by association. A good example of this is in households that have more than one dog.

The new dog will pick up the good (and bad) behaviors of the dogs already in the house. A pup may learn the *sit* completely by watching the older dog *sit* for treats. He will even learn the verbal command. So, for behaviors that a dog can naturally produce, the method of learning by association can be a good training tool to add to your bag of tricks.

Capturing To train a GSD to provide a behavior without luring him

into the behavior, simply wait. When the dog shows the desired behavior, link the voice command with the final action of producing the behavior and reward. For example, if your GSD is circling to lie down, as he lies down, say the command, *"Down!"* and reward when he is in the down position. This can be done with focusing on you (*Here*), *sit, down, come,* etc.

The only problem with this method is that it is not efficient because you can only link a verbal command with the behavior when the dog produces the behavior on his own. Additionally, this method is not useable when the behavior you seek is not produced by the dog naturally or is a complex, multistep behavior.

Reinforcements: What They Are and How They Work

Dogs respond to positive training methods. A key to positive reinforcement training is the use of a reward system to reinforce specific behaviors. What you choose to use as a reinforcement is dependent on your GSD.

Value of a treat Often, owners will use a training treat that is convenient and that their GSDs show interest in. For many GSDs, this could be anything that resembles food. A treat is good, but the treat that your GSD would jump through rings of fire to get is the treat you really want to use when training. Using a lesser-valued treat is okay, but you will lose your pup's attention as he matures. The GSD was bred to pick up and focus on small movements. Therefore, the lesser treat will no longer work to keep his focus when he encounters differences in surroundings and sounds. You will need to work with the high-value treat to get the best results. So, as you begin your training journey, pay attention to the effect different treats have on your GSD.

Other types of reinforcements What if your GSD is not a food hound and not even bits of grilled chicken or sliced filet mignon will do the trick? Is he a ball fiend? K-9s are often trained with a ball on a rope because many working dogs are so ball crazy that they shake with excitement when they see the ball. Does he prefer a tug toy? Is he squeaker crazy? It won't take long working with a high-drive dog to discover what toy makes your dog want to do whatever it takes to get what you have. When you find the right toy, use this as his incentive to produce the behaviors you want.

Verbal/physical praise Your voice and your patting are highly-valued as rewards by the dog that has a very close working/companion bond with his owner/handler. Praise, both verbal and physical, is always a good reward; however, you will not able to use praise as a physical lure to shape behaviors or to get a

dog salivating in anticipation of THE reward. With that said, verbal and physical praise should always be a part of your training program.

A Question of Timing

When rewarding a behavior, timing is critical. The reward must be instantaneous with the completion of the behavior you've asked your GSD to provide. That way, he will link the reward with the behavior. If the reward is given four seconds later, your GSD will associate the reward with the behavior *at that time*—not the behavior he gave you four seconds prior.

For example, your GSD does a *sit*. You praise him as he is breaking the *sit* to do something else. Now you've just reinforced breaking the *sit*, not the *sit* itself. To link the *sit* with the reward, reward the pup immediately upon his full and complete *sit*. Now you've rewarded the behavior you want, not a different behavior entirely.

Linking the verbal command with the desired behavior is also dependent on timing. To ensure, for example, that the command *"Sit!"* is linked with the act of sitting, and not a squat or a partial sit, it is imperative to teach the behavior of sitting first using lures and positive reinforcement. Once the dog *knows* the behavior (in this example, the *sit*) and consistently produces the behavior, the verbal command can be linked with the behavior.

When linking the verbal command, say the command when you're 99.99 percent positive he will complete the behavior. Using the *sit* as an example, the verbal command would be given *just as his haunches hit the ground.* Later, the command *"Sit!"* can be given when he's halfway through his *sit*. Finally, as he links the act of sitting with the verbal command, you will be able to say *"Sit!"* when you are looking at him and have his focus, and he will immediately *sit*.

No hesitation rule When teaching commands and linking them to behaviors, do not assume your GSD has linked the verbal command with the behavior. If you move too quickly when linking the word for the command (e.g., *sit*) with the action of sitting, your GSD can become confused. Your GSD is uncertain what to do if he is producing the behavior slowly and is watching your physical, non-verbal cues. If you find he is not completing the behavior quickly, make the exercise easier until he is providing the behavior swiftly and with confidence.

No repeat rule If you say *"Sit, sit, sit, sit, SIT!!"* before your GSD actually sits, you've just taught him that he can wait to hear the command four or five times before he has to *sit*. Your GSD does not have a hearing problem. He would hear you if you whispered. He has a training problem in that you've trained him that he can wait to *sit*.

If he doesn't provide the behavior you've given him the command for, *do not repeat the command*. Pull out your lure, lure him into the behavior you want, and relink the verbal command. Reward. Repeat until he is fast and sure of himself. Then work backward, linking the verbal command earlier and earlier.

Benefits of a Great Trainer and Training School

You can train your GSD on your own and this book will give you the basics to get you started. But, what a book can't do is watch your handling and your dog's responses and determine training issues or ways to improve your dog's responses. If you work with an experienced GSD trainer, training your GSD goes more quickly and progresses with less training errors. Your trainer will be able to read your puppy, adult, or rescue quickly and know the best approaches to training your GSD. Your trainer also will recognize any potential behavior issues your dog has and will devise a training plan to address them before they develop or worsen. Working with a knowledgeable trainer enables you to become a more skilled trainer. Your trainer will show you methods that will work with your dog. Your trainer will help you improve your timing for rewards and linking verbal commands. And, your trainer will physically be able to show you what he or she is telling you to do with your puppy or dog. He or she will also become a lifelong resource

for problem-solving with your dog, including problem-solving for behaviors in the home, and reassurance that what you are seeing are typical dog behaviors that are rectifiable and not some embodiment of Cujo.

Another valuable benefit of working with a trainer is that if he or she runs a training school, you and your GSD will be able to work on socialization skills, including people socialization and dog-dog socialization.

Finding a Good Trainer/Training School

Dog training seems to be a popular profession as of late, and the abilities, experience, and skill set of dog trainers runs the gamut of outstanding to less than stellar. With the German Shepherd Dog, it is important that the trainer with whom you are working is first and foremost a trainer who believes in positive, reward-based training methods. Second, the trainer should have extensive working dog experience. Yes, the GSD is classified as a herding breed but because of his long history of working in a variety of military, police, tracking, service, and other working activities, it is important that your trainer understands the unique courage, determination, drives, and specific characteristics of the working dog—as well as the absolute need for exercise and mental stimulation. The GSD has very specific characteristics, temperaments, and drives that are unlike most other dogs.

When looking for a trainer, ask what breeds he or she has worked with. What breed does he or she personally train and compete with? (Bonus points if the trainer works with GSDs.) German Shepherd Dogs are the No. 2 most popular breed in the country, so you should be able to find a trainer who completely understands this breed, its attributes, and its challenges. Also, pay attention to the source of trainer recommendations. Ask the GSD Rescue in your area who they recommend for training. Adult GSD rescue dogs usually

have not had any training and come with their own unique set of issues, so the breed rescues typically work with trainers to evaluate the temperament and training knowledge/abilities of the dogs they are fostering.

If your breeder is local, ask him or her for trainer referrals. Ask other dog owners that you know and admire for their well-trained dogs.

Ask your veterinarian for suggestions. With many puppies coming through the clinics, most veterinarians have a feel for training schools, as they have seen the before (puppy) and after (adult dog) of those who have gone through local training schools and trainers.

Once you have a short list of recommended trainers and training schools, check out some training classes in person. Talk to the clients. See what everyone is doing in the class. Is it a good fit for you and your dog? Are the clients and dogs happy and having fun? What kind of collars are they using? (Answer: not choke, prong, or shock collars.) Do you feel as if you could work with this trainer? Do you feel you would be comfortable asking this trainer a lot of questions? The best trainer in the world is not a good choice for you if you aren't completely comfortable working with him or her.

Bottom line: Trust your gut. If you're uncomfortable in any way, it doesn't matter if this is the first puppy you've ever trained, trust yourself. If you're not comfortable, your dog won't be either. Keep looking. You will find a good school.

Home-Schooling: Clicker Training Basics

Clicker training enables the trainer to pinpoint the moment the dog gives a correct behavior and reward it with an intermediary reward—the sound of the clicker. Clicker training can be particularly helpful when teaching dogs very complex, multistep behaviors, such as training a service dog to go to the refrigerator, open the door, remove a chilled medication, shut the door, and bring the medication to the handler. In this example, the clicker is used to reward each segment of the entire multistep trained behavior.

Conditioning the dog to the clicker: For clicker training to work, the dog must realize that a "click" means he did something right and a treat is coming. To link the "treat is coming" with the "click," hold the clicker in one hand and a pile of treats in the other. With your dog's focus on you, click and immediately treat. Repeat until all the treats are gone. In short order, the dog will associate the click with receiving a reward.

Once the dog understands that the clicker means a treat is coming, you can use the clicker at the same time as you would give verbal praise followed by a treat/toy reward. Once the dog has linked the verbal command with the behavior, the clicker is gradually removed from the training of that behavior, just as a treat reward is gradually removed.

Clicking can be overdone and dogs can become immune to the sound of the click. Using a clicker also requires the availability of both hands while holding a leash or using a lure to shape a behavior. Timing is critical with the sounding of the "click," so if training with a clicker is of interest to you, it is advisable to work with a trainer who is an expert in this technique.

For a good resource on clicker training, check out *Clicker Training for Obedience*, by Morgan Spector.

Chapter Eight

Commands Your German Shepherd Dog Needs to Know

If you only teach your GSD three commands, they should be *"Here," "Sit,"* and *"Come."* Of course, just as you can play a round of golf with three clubs (a driver, a putter, and a 7 iron), that doesn't mean you should or that your game will be admirable.

The more commands your GSD knows and performs, the more versatile he will be. He will be fun to live with, he will be better in unexpected or unusual circumstances, and it will be easier to maintain a healthy level of socialization with people and around other dogs.

So, let's get started!

Here or *Watch Me*

This command is used to train your GSD to immediately pay attention, lock eyes, and anticipate additional orders from you. The *here* command should be taught as soon as you bring home your GSD, regardless of his age. Until your GSD has mastered the *here* command, it is something you can work on throughout the day.

Your goal is to gain your GSD's intense focus on you the moment you give him your chosen "focus" command. It can be *"Here," "Watch Me," "Look,"* or another word of your choice. Ultimately, you will want him to focus on you with that one word, no matter where he is or what he is doing—even if you are completely out of sight. If he hears his "focus" word, he knows to find you and be immediately ready for your next command.

Hint: Although many people choose to use the words, *"Watch Me,"* for this exercise, the word *"Here"* is an even better choice. Single word or one-syllable commands are short, making them easier for the dog to learn. Avoid words that sound similar, as sound-alike words (i.e., *"find"* and *"phone"*) could be confusing to a dog. Whatever word you choose, the *here* command will result in your dog focusing on you

and what is coming next. It is an important command during socialization, and a dog that is trained with a focus command will learn to run to you when he hears the command, because to him, the command requires him to be close to you and making direct eye contact.

Method
- **Step 1:** With a bag of your dog's favorite, motivational treats in hand, wait for your GSD to make direct eye contact and say, "*Here!*" Reward the GSD immediately. Continue to do this throughout the day.
- **Step 2:** When you are confident that your GSD has linked the verbal command with the action of

locking eyes with you, look for opportunities when he is not quite looking at you but you are confident when you speak, he will look at you. Say, "*Here!*" and reward when he turns to look directly at you. Repeat throughout the day.
- **Step 3:** Make the exercise harder by giving him the focus command when he's farther away and looking at you or nearby and slightly distracted. Give the *here* command and reward him when he turns to look directly at you. Repeat and continue to make it a little bit harder each day.
- **Step 4:** Increase the distractions he has when you give the command by taking him outside. When you do this, it is very impor-

tant that you start from Step 1, and make this exercise easy for him to succeed at. In other words, when adding difficulty to the exercise either by more distractions, or more distance, start at the beginning level of the exercise to "reteach" the command when it's harder for him to focus on you. In this way, you are setting him up to succeed by bringing the exercise to a level where he can easily get the behavior right.

What you don't want to do is add difficulty to the exercise and have your dog not respond or become confused. If this happens (he doesn't respond), take the reward that he can't live without (the $125/hour reward), bring it to his nose, raise the treat up to your eyes, say "*Here!*" then immediately reward him. Repeat and reward. Continue to lure with the treat until he's made the connection again, and then go back to making the exercise incrementally more difficult.

- **Step 5:** When he is consistently focusing on you with mild distractions outdoors, take him to a more distracting place. Build up from Step 1 again.

Collar Touch

A bounding, jumping, fast-moving GSD that won't let you grab his collar is no fun. Nimble, big, and quick, the GSD is going to win this game

Stop on a Good Note

Your German Shepherd Dog is a fast learner that enjoys mental stimulation. He also loves being with you, so training is a fun activity for him. If you are working with a young GSD, keep the sessions short and interspersed throughout the day. If your German Shepherd Dog is older, he can maintain focus and train for longer periods of time.

Remember, regardless of how long you train your dog, do not extend the training session after you've lost your GSD's attention. Ideally, you will want to quit your training session with your puppy or dog wanting more. You want him to be anxious to train again.

If you accidently train too long and your GSD is losing interest or is mentally or physically tired, find that *one thing* he can do well, such as a *sit,* give him the command, reward, and release. Praise him enthusiastically and then quit. Always finish on a good note.

every single time. To avoid this evasive game, and to make your GSD "collar approachable" by other people, teach your GSD the *collar touch*. The first time he gets loose and someone else grabs him by the collar to snap on a leash—or at least hold him until you can get there—you'll appreciate the fact that your German Shepherd Dog accepts this skill from strangers.

Method

- **Step 1:** Have treats in hand ready to reward.
- **Step 2:** With your GSD next to you—and with his leash slack but clipped onto his collar—touch his collar. If he bounces away, use the treat to lure him closer and touch his collar.
- **Step 3:** Reward him immediately with the treat every time he allows you to touch his collar. Repeat, reward. Work on this exercise daily.
- **Step 4:** Put him in a *sit* (see, "*Sit*," page 99) with a known friend/family member holding his leash loosely. Have the friend or family member pet the GSD and then hold a treat and touch the dog's collar.
- **Step 5:** Have the friend reward the dog.
- **Step 6:** Increase difficulty by having the friend reach out and hold (rather than touch) the GSD's collar.
- **Step 7:** Repeat and reward.

Sit

The uses and practicality of the *sit* command are so great that if you teach just one command, it needs to be the *sit*. You'll use the *sit* throughout the day and every day for the entirety of your dog's life. (If you're lucky, your puppy may have been taught the *sit* by his breeder.) Your GSD can learn the *sit* quickly no matter what age he is.

Use the *sit* to teach your happy puppy or boisterous dog to *sit* to receive treats and attention from strangers. The *sit* should be used when you are preparing your GSD's food and you don't want him to jump up and knock the bowl out of your hands. The *sit* can be used to help calm an overstimulated GSD when playing with other dogs (think of it as a calming time-out). And, if you're having problems with your GSD jumping up, bolting out the front door, or running away when you need to clip the leash onto his collar before you take him for a walk, use the *sit*.

Training the *sit* is simple when you use a treat or other highly motivational reward as a lure.

Method
- **Step 1:** Get your GSD's attention with the *here* command.
- **Step 2:** Lightly holding his collar, or with your leash clipped onto his collar, take your treat and place it right in front of his nose.
- **Step 3:** Move the treat from his nose tip to between his ears in one, slow motion. He should fold backward into a *sit*.
- **Step 4:** Reward him. Repeat. Practice this exercise every chance you get during the day. Keep practicing until all you do is hold the treat and he folds into a *sit*.
- **Step 5:** Link the command, "*Sit!*" with the motion of sitting. As your GSD is finishing his sit (still using the lure), say, "*Sit!*" as he finishes the act of sitting. Reward. Repeat.

Note: This is not linking the verbal command, "*Sit!*" with the motion of your hand. You want your GSD to *sit* without any hand movement when you link the verbal command, "*Sit!*" By linking the action of sitting (and not the luring motion of your hand) with the verbal command, "*Sit!*" your GSD will not be dependent on a hand

degree of difficulty with the distractions at the new location requires that you break the exercise back down to the basics, so your dog has the greatest chance of succeeding. He should pick up quickly within the first few times of luring him into the *sit*. If he doesn't "get it"—are you using a super high-value treat? This is the time that you need something that he would jump through rings of fire to have. Make sure you have his focus. If he can't focus on you, take him back to a location with few distractions and rebuild the exercise.

- **Step 8:** If at any time he doesn't *sit* with confidence and speed, back up the exercise to something simpler with fewer distractions, less movement, or less distance. Take the exercise back to a point at which you know he will *sit,* and build the exercise back up before adding a degree of difficulty.

motion (cue) to *sit.* Your goal is to be able to give the *sit* command and even if he can't see you, he will still *sit.*

- **Step 6:** Link the voice command sooner in the act of sitting. Reward. Repeat. Your goal is to say *"Sit!"* while you have your dog's attention (but he is standing) and he immediately folds into a *sit.*

    Note: If he doesn't *sit*, do not repeat the command! Pull out your treat, reshape the *sit* with the lure, and say the command as he is finishing the act of sitting. Repeat the beginning steps until he is sitting quickly and confidently.

- **Step 7:** Make the exercise more challenging by taking your GSD to a new place with more distractions. When you are at the new location, it is important to begin with Steps 1 through 4. Yes, you are "retraining" the *sit*, but the

Stay

If your GSD has mastered the *sit* command, the *sit-stay* is the next skill you'll want your GSD to have in his arsenal of commands that he knows and performs flawlessly. The *stay* is good to use to calm your dog (in a *down-stay*), to prevent him from jumping out of the car the moment you open the door (*sit-stay* or *down-stay*), to keep him on the top step of your stairs while you walk to the bottom without him pulling you down the stairs (*sit-stay*), to keep him from pushing first through doorways in your home (*sit-stay*), and to have him rest calmly at your feet while you eat al fresco at a restaurant (*down-stay*).

Method
- **Step 1:** With his leash on, his attention on you, and standing at your left side, put your GSD in a *sit*.
- **Step 2:** With your left hand directly in front of his nose, move your hand in a short right to left motion, fingers down toward the floor and palm toward your dog, and say, "*Stay!*"
- **Step 3:** Stand next to your dog for five seconds without either of you moving.
- **Step 4:** Release your dog ("OK!") and reward.
- **Step 5:** Repeat steps 1–4, releasing after every few *sit-stays*.

- **Step 6:** Make the exercise harder by doing one of these:
  a. Keeping the dog in a *stay* for increasingly longer periods of time, or
  b. Keeping the dog in a *stay* while you take one step to the right away from your dog and come right back. Take a step backward and come right back. Take a step forward and come right back.
- **Step 7:** Continue to make the exercise harder by increasing *one* of these factors:
  a. Time that the dog is in a *stay.*
  b. Distance that you walk from the dog while he is in a *stay.*
  c. Distractions that occur while your dog is in a *stay.*
  d. Add motion and odd positions: Jump up and down, squat, turn your back to him, etc. If at any time he breaks his *stay*, put him back in a *sit*, make the exercise simpler, and build back up to the point where he became confused.

Down

The *down* is a helpful command that teaches your dog gentle leadership skills. The *down* is viewed as a submissive position by most dogs, and having your dog *down* will reinforce that you are the leader in a gentle and kind manner. Additionally, it is hard for many dogs to bark from the *down*. Of course, this won't stop your GSD from whining and talking while he is in a *down*, but it will help with the barking. The *down* is also a helpful tool that can be used in settling your dog, as lying down is the first step toward taking a nap.

Method
- **Step 1:** Put your dog in a *sit*. He should be facing you and have his leash clipped to his collar.
- **Step 2:** With your high-value treat or reinforcement in your right hand, move your hand from his nose, straight down to the floor and hold the treat on the floor. He should follow the treat and drop quickly to the floor. If he raises his haunches (rear) in the air instead of dropping completely to the floor, put him back in a *sit*, and repeat the process.
- **Step 3:** Continue luring him to the floor until he is dropping to the floor without hesitation or raising his haunches in the air.
- **Step 4:** When he is luring well into his *down*, watch for a hip rollover. A rolled hip is a more comfortable, relaxed *down* position. The *down,* in which he is lying down but looking like he could spring at any moment, is a more temporary *down*.

Using the Capturing method described on page 87, when you see your puppy or adult GSD relax in his *down* to the point of rolling over his hip, reward him. You want to encourage the rolled hip, relaxed, "long-term" *down.*
- **Step 5:** Link the voice command *"Down!"* with the action of lying down. Lure him into a *down*. Reward and repeat until he is link-

ing the word "*Down!*" with the action of finishing a *down*. Keep backing up the verbal command link earlier and earlier in the actual luring of the *down* until you can say "*Down!*" when he is in a *sit*, and he can lie down and roll his hip. Continue praising, rewarding, and practicing.

- **Step 6:** Make it harder. Add distractions in a distraction-free place, such as give the *down* command with family members present, or a family pet present but separated, or while you're preparing his dinner. If at any time the GSD is slow in his *down* or doesn't *down* immediately on command, go back to Steps 1–4 to reteach the *down* without distractions.

- **Step 7:** Continue to take him to different places and work on the *down*.

Come

The recall, or *come* command, can be a lifesaver. If your dog accidently gets loose from an open gate in the yard, you can use the *come* command, and be confident that he will return immediately to you. If you are hiking and see wildlife that your GSD absolutely must not confront (and that would be all wildlife), you can recall your GSD and be assured he will return safely to you. Recalls are helpful in multi-dog situations when one or more dogs are getting overstimulated and need to come out of the play area and cool down, too.

For the recall to work, however, you must practice this exercise regularly, and it is equally as important that your practice is as near to perfect as you can get it. This is one exercise in particular that the GSD must be set up to succeed at every single time because if he learns just once that he doesn't have to come when you say, "*Come!*" it will take many, many repetitions of requiring him to come to you to erase that one instance when he didn't.

Also, it is important not to get in the habit of giving the command, *"Come!"* multiple times. Repeating a command will teach your GSD that he doesn't have to respond until he hears you shout the final *"Come!"* with your neck arteries bulging. And, at that point, he may realize he's better off *not* coming to you, which is what happens if you give the recall command to punish your dog. For example, you shout *"Come!"* and when he does come, you scold him for taking five commands to come to you. Guess what you've just taught your GSD? If he comes, he will be punished. Guess which dog will not come when called . . . ever?

To avoid ever falling into these bad habits and imperfect training, follow these steps:

Method

- **Step 1:** Be in the correct frame of mind: never angry, tired, or grouchy. Your mood will affect your GSD's willingness to come to you. Keep it happy, joyful, and above all *fun.* The recall is always reward-based.
- **Step 2:** Make sure your GSD is rock solid on his *down-stay* before beginning any recall training.
- **Step 3:** With your GSD on leash, give a *down-stay*, walk away from him, and come right back.
- **Step 4:** Walk away again, and then say *"Come!"* Be enthusiastic. Encourage the dog to come to you. Give an ever so slight tug on

the leash to encourage your dog to break his *down-stay* and start running toward you.

Note: This leash "tug" is like a very light tap on the shoulder. It is barely there, but it is enough for your GSD to say, "Oh! We're doing something different here!" It is *not* a pull, or a pop, or a drag. It is simply a barely-there, super light, split-second tug.

- **Step 5:** Run backward to encourage him to come to you faster.
- **Step 6:** Reward him like crazy for coming to you. Play.
- **Step 7:** Repeat steps 1 through 5.
- **Step 8:** Make the exercise more challenging. Loop two leashes together and walk 12 feet (4 yards) away from him for the recall. Reward like crazy. Keep it fun and keep him on leash.
- **Step 9:** Work on the recall in unfamiliar places on leash. If he forgets and tries to run off toward a distraction, use gentle tugs and a very high-value lure to get him back on track. Practice, reward, and keep working on it.
- **Step 10:** Begin off-leash recalls. Initially, practice these in an area with little to no distractions. Know your Plan B: If he doesn't come to you and runs off, what are you going to do? You must be able to catch him easily, put him back on leash, and work from the ground up again. Any "failure to *come*" with this exercise will require a very long time to rebuild a reliable off-leash recall again. Do not practice an off-leash recall until

your GSD is solid on a long line in virtually every place imaginable. Do not practice an off-leash recall in an area that is not fenced.

Tip: Add his name to the recall ("*Rock, Come!*") if you are in an area with other dogs, for example, and your GSD needs to know you are recalling *him*.

Heel

"Heeling" is an obedience skill that is used in competitive obedience trials, as well as other performance dog events. The *heel* requires

that the dog stay precisely at your side with his shoulder next to your leg. If you speed up, he speeds up. If you slow down, he slows down. If you turn right, he turns right. If you turn left, he turns left. If you stop, he snaps to a *sit.* It is a precision behavior that in competition, the slightest surge forward or lag behind is penalized.

Teaching the *heel* enables you to take a leisurely walk with your dog in which he is on a loose, slack leash getting his "sniff on" in a relaxed human-dog bond, but if you need to, you can tell him "*Heel!*" and he will immediately fall in at your side and give you his complete attention. Being able to put a dog on a *heel* at any time allows you to be proactive. If you are in an area with a lot of people or other dogs, you can put your dog in a *heel* and know that he will be glued to your left leg without lunging ahead, stopping to check something out, or becoming overstimulated with other dogs around. His focus will be on you, and he will be in control, so you can stop worrying about weaving your way through crowded situations without tripping someone with your errant GSD and his leash.

Method

- **Step 1:** Make sure you have your dog's attention and focus. Use the "*Here!*" command if needed.
- **Step 2:** Hold his high-value treat or toy in your right hand.
- **Step 3:** Put your GSD on your left side.

- **Step 4:** Move your right arm across your hips so that your hand is slightly protruding on the left, where your dog is.
- **Step 5:** Step out with your *left* foot first (this is his signal to move forward with you), keeping that item of value on your left hip in your hand.
- **Step 6:** Say, "*Heel!*" Reward for staying glued to your left side.
- **Step 7:** Practice, practice, practice. Add changes of pace—faster, slower. Add turns. Keep rewarding good work.
- **Step 8:** Gradually, as his heeling becomes solid, take away the lure. If at any time he loses position, becomes distracted, etc., go back to the initial steps, using the lure and build back up to where he fell apart a little.

Other heeling considerations: Keep the leash loose: Your GSD needs to be in position and heeling with you on his own free will. A tight leash is uncomfortable for the dog and shouldn't be used to force or keep the dog in position. It's a similar feeling to someone holding onto the back of your shirt while you are trying to walk. A tight leash can also relay anxieties to the dog; you do not want your dog looking for something to protect you from. With a loose leash, your GSD will continue to focus on you for direction; he will keep glancing up and looking at you. Keep it friendly and fun and he will be a joyous, happy heeler.

Chapter Nine
Additional Helpful Commands

Off and *Up*

The *off* command is used to signal your GSD to jump out of a car or truck, or off a couch, chair, or bed. This command can help prevent a potential confrontation with an older puppy or an adult dog that is showing dominant, yellow-light behaviors while refusing to leave a comfortable spot on the couch or bed. If the GSD knows the *off* command, this confrontation can be avoided.

Up is used for the reverse of *off* and is the command you would use to get your GSD to jump into the car or truck, or jump up on a specific surface (such as the pause table in agility). The *off* and *up* commands can be taught at the same time.

Note: Many dog owners use the verbal command, "*Down!*" when they really mean *off*. Using *down* for the motion of a dog jumping off something is confusing for the dog and can cause issues when you use *down* to mean what you've originally taught him to do: lie down.

When He Doesn't Budge

Tip: If your GSD refuses to jump off the bed or other surface, rather than attempting to physically move him, get your leash and a treat. Snap the leash on his collar (or if he is being really confrontational, make a lasso from the leash and loop it over his head *or* simply use a high-value treat and avoid his collar/head area completely). Use a high-value treat as a lure. Have him *sit* when he is off the bed. Wait a few seconds and then reward him. Then, make a conscious effort to work on the *off* command.

Method
- **Step 1:** With your GSD on leash and a high-value reward in hand, select a surface for your GSD to jump on and off without much effort. For a puppy, make sure the surface is low and easy for him to jump on and off, such as a seat cushion from the couch. For adult GSDs, use something, such as a low couch or chair, that has a non-slick surface.

Retrieving a Guarded Item Safely

If you haven't taught your GSD the *out* command, you need to be prepared to keep a calm and level head and do the following to get him to release the item he is guarding:

- **Step 1:** Find an object that is of an even higher value to him than the object he is guarding. **Note:** This may not be possible, but make the effort to have a high-value treat in hand.
- **Step 2:** If he is guarding the item, it is too dangerous to clip a leash on him at this point. Make a loop with your leash and lasso your GSD.
- **Step 3:** Offer the high-value item as a swap. **Note:** if he is truly guarding the item, he will not give up the item and his guarding behaviors may escalate.
- **Step 4:** If he drops the item he is guarding in exchange for the high-value treat, *quickly* pull him away from the item. Put him in a *sit*. Make sure you are far enough away from the item that he can't snap the guarded item back up. Reward him for calm behavior only while he is in the *sit*.
- **Step 4** Alternative: If he won't swap the item, say, "*Let's go for a walk!*" and see if walking him directly to the door will cause him to drop the item. If he does, do not allow him to snap it back up. Finish with steps 5 and 6. If he still won't drop the item, take him on a walk. Continue with a training session until he drops the item.
- **Step 5:** Move him to a place, such as his crate, where he can't retrieve the item.
- **Step 6:** Remove the object and throw it away *permanently*.

    Note: Whatever the item was that he was guarding, he is never to have it again. If it was a certain kind of bone or chew, don't buy that bone or chew again. If it was a household object, make sure he does not have access to it again.
- **Step 7:** Teach him the *take it* and *out* commands.

- **Step 2:** Use the treat or toy to lure your GSD up on the surface you've selected. Reward.
- **Step 3:** Use the treat or toy to lure your GSD off the surface.

    Note: If your GSD is not following the lure, and you are using a high-value treat, could your GSD have a joint issue that is making it painful for him to jump up or down? If a GSD was previously capable of jumping up and down from surfaces but is now reluctant, consider a health check at the veterinarian to examine him for hip dysplasia or elbow dysplasia that could be causing him pain.

- **Step 4:** Link the verbal commands "*Up!*" and "*Off!*" with the actions of jumping up and down.
- **Step 5:** Make the exercise more difficult. Train using higher surfaces (within the GSD's physical capabilities). Train in different environments.
- **Step 6:** Transition the GSD's training to the car or truck. Begin with the lure and have the car or truck in a location with few distractions. As he jumps in and out easily, continue luring when the car or truck is in an area with distractions. When the dog is solid and quick with his responses to the verbal commands, begin reducing the use of lures.

Stand

The *stand* command is helpful if you are considering showing your GSD in conformation classes, in which the dog is required to *stand* for examination and in the "line up" for the judge to evaluate the dogs. The *stand* command will also be used if you are considering competing in obedience trials with your dog. For example, in the *Companion Dog,* or first level of AKC obedience, one of the exercises is a *stand for examination*. Additionally, the *stand* can be used while grooming your GSD, as it's much easier to brush his coat and trim his nails if he is standing.

Method
- **Step 1:** With the leash attached, put your dog in a *sit.*
- **Step 2:** With a gentle and ever so slight forward motion of the leash, to encourage your dog to stand up, lead him into a *stand.*
- **Step 3:** Quickly catch your GSD under his tuck up/tummy area with your left hand so he won't sit and say *"Stand!"*
- **Step 4:** Hold him in position so he understands the behavior you want.
- **Step 5:** Reward and release him with *"OK!"*

- **Step 6:** Practice. Eventually discontinue scooping up his tummy as he figures out the *stand.*
- **Step 7:** Make it more difficult by making him stand for longer periods of time; work the *stand* into a *stand-stay.* Have him stand in areas with more distractions, but be sure to go back to steps 1–5 when in a new location.
- **Step 8:** Have him stand while a trusted person examines his teeth, legs, topline, and tail.

Take It and *Out*

The question is not "if" but "when" your GSD puppy, adult, or rescue picks up an item that he is either not supposed to have (i.e., your shoe, a child's toy, an entire roll of toilet paper, etc.) or an item that is dangerous for him to have (i.e., a tin can, a plastic pill vial containing medicine, a bottle of wood glue, etc.). In that moment, you need him to drop the item and you need him to drop the item immediately. This is not the time for the GSD to play a game of chase me, nor is it the time for your GSD to display the red-light behaviors of resource guarding. If you've taught him the *out* command, retrieving the GSD's treasure will be no problem.

Method
- **Step 1:** Find an object that he likes and can hold in his mouth.
- **Step 2:** Have his high-value treat/toy on hand. If he is crazy for

balls, this exercise can be done with two favorite balls.

- **Step 3:** With your GSD on leash, offer him the object that he likes to hold in his mouth.
- **Step 4:** Say *"Take it!"* as he takes the toy.
- **Step 5:** Offer him the high-value treat to drop the toy. As he drops the toy, say, *"Out!"*
- **Step 6:** Reward him with the treat. Practice.
- **Step 7:** Make it more difficult. When he is easily performing *take it* and *out* consistently, quickly and without the high-value reward, try having him "take" different types and textures of objects, such as a wooden dumbbell or a metal dumbbell (dogs don't enjoy holding metal in their mouths). Or, you can increase the difficulty by using the original objects that you taught him with but take him to an area with more distractions.
- **Step 8:** Remember to go back to steps 1 through 5 when increasing the difficulty of the exercise.

Leave It

The *leave it* command can be used for any instance in which you want your GSD to ignore something. The *leave it* command means: don't touch it, don't eat it, don't taste it, don't acknowledge it, or don't chase it.

Method

- **Step 1:** With your GSD on leash, walk.
- **Step 2:** When something distracts your GSD, give him a light correction (very slight pull) on the leash.
- **Step 3:** Say *"Leave it!"* when you give him the light correction.
- **Step 4:** Immediately treat/reward him.
- **Step 5:** If your walk doesn't have many distractions, you can work on this with "planted" items— things that you think might distract him—such as a paper plate, a toy, a small piece of food, etc. Make sure you have a high-value reward in hand, one that he values more than the distraction.

Chapter Ten

Preventing Problem Behaviors

As noted in the opening chapters, the GSD is a herding dog with working abilities and characteristics. As such, he was bred for endurance and is highly motivated. He is exceptionally intelligent and has the tendency to run the household if no one else steps forward.

Because of these characteristics, the GSD requires a lot of exercise, intense and daily mental stimulation, as well as constant and consistent leadership.

The Importance of Exercise and Mental Stimulation

When he doesn't get a sufficient amount of exercise and mental stimulation, things happen. And, they are never good things. A GSD's idea of occupying himself is disastrous for all involved. He *will* play interior decorator and tear up couches, scratch walls, remove door frames, or perhaps even remove the door itself.

Don't think crating your destructive GSD is the solution either. Over-crating an active GSD that is in desperate need of exercise and/or mental stimulation creates a GSD with serious anxiety issues that can manifest in self-destruction.

It is much easier to keep your GSD well exercised and mentally challenged. Some ways to accomplish the exercise factor include regular long runs, walks, and open-area play (in a fenced-in area). To address the mental stimulation factor, the

GSD's daily regime should include obedience training, play with interactive toys where he has to figure out the puzzle to retrieve the snack, and throwing a ball into deep grass, which requires the dog to find the ball using his scenting ability.

Even with plenty of exercise and mental stimulation, a GSD can acquire bad habits. It is easier to be proactive in recognizing potential issues before they become bad habits than it is to break a bad habit. But, sometimes even with the best of intentions, some undesirable behaviors form. The following are guidelines on preventing, as well as correcting, typical "bad" GSD behaviors.

Mouthing

When a puppy is teething, from four to six months, your GSD will require safe, healthy chew toys to satiate his need to chew. Good choices include:

- Kongs stuffed with peanut butter and frozen: freezing makes them last longer, as well as relieves the itchy, swollen gums that go along with losing teeth and erupting molars.
- Nylabones—another tough chew toy that can be frozen, too, if desired.
- Heavy, hard-rubber toys that cannot be swallowed whole or do not have small pieces that can be gnawed off and potentially cause the pup to choke.

- Frozen towels—this item requires close supervision, and the towel must be taken away before the pup starts to shred it.

When mouthing of a teething puppy turns into mouthing from an adolescent dog, it is not fun. It is a behavior that must be stopped before it becomes more serious and leads to bites.

Refrain from saying "*Ow!*" in a high-pitched voice: this *does not* work with the GSD. This is a breed that whines and yip-barks to gain attention and to communicate—so the high-pitched "*Ow!*" does not work with him. In fact, a high-pitched voice is a *praise* voice for the GSD. If you yelp, "*Ow!*" you've just rewarded him for nipping you.

Method 1: Stop all play and ignore him. By not responding and ignoring him, you've effectively given him a negative reinforcement—the withholding of attention.

Method 2: With a lower, in-charge voice, say "*Ah, Ah!*"

Keep Calm

Do not tell him "*Stop it,*" "*No,*" etc., in a high-pitched voice, which most of us use when we are angry! Remember, a high-pitched voice is a praise voice. A praise voice will encourage him to continue barking.

Method 3: If the GSD is over-the-top with his nipping, and he is a bold, not easily put off, dog (and not a soft, reactive, or very sensitive dog), then you can consider using a shaker can. A shaker can is a tin can with a few pennies in it or other offensive noisemaking items.

- **Step 1:** Set up a situation in which you know he will try to nip you. For example, if you know he will try to nip when you're on the couch, have the shaker can with you, as well as high-value rewards.
- **Step 2:** When he is in the act of nipping you, shake the can. Keep in mind that it shouldn't be an enormous, super-scary noise. It is just supposed to be something that he finds a little uncomfortable.
- **Step 3:** When he doesn't nip and is settled, reward him.
- **Step 4:** Practice.

Barking/Whining

GSDs are naturally very vocal. They have a high-pitched whine that defies normal patience levels and is a comparable sensation to sandpaper on your soul. The GSD is also capable of some serious barking, all of which can drive an owner bonkers. The following are some approaches to lessen his vocalizations.

First, make sure your dog is well-exercised and mentally stimulated. Excessive vocalizations can be a sign of a bored or pent-up GSD.

Second, look at how your home is set up. Is he barking at people from a window as they walk by your home? Or is he barking at delivery people through a sidelight as they approach the front door? These behaviors are self-rewarding behaviors in that the GSD is rewarded for his barking: The person leaves the property. Never mind that the GSD had nothing to do with the person leaving because in his mind, he *did that*.

So, if your GSD can see everything that goes on in front of your home and is incessantly barking (an alert bark is fine—you want him to be able to watch, but you want him to be reasonable and not work himself up into a yellow- or even a red-light behavior), keep him away from your front door, especially when you are not home to tell him *"Enough."*

If your puppy or adult dog is yipping, whining, and barking in his crate, you can follow these tips to quiet a noisy GSD.

- If you are certain he doesn't have to relieve himself, ignore him. Say nothing. Reward him when he's quiet and only when he's quiet, then walk away again. Reward when he's quite again. Remember that letting him out of the crate is a reward, too.
- Do not try to soothe your puppy or dog. Again, the GSD hears the high-pitched voice as a reward. Don't do it. You will make your problem worse.
- Provide your GSD with safe chews in his crate. These can act as pacifiers to occupy him. And, if he is busy with his mouth, he is less likely to be yipping and whining.
- Make sure you've given him enough exercise and mental stimulation throughout the day. This can't be emphasized enough, as the GSD is exceptionally active both physically and mentally. If these needs are not met, he will vocalize his boredom and his need to exercise.

Teaching *Quiet*

Be forewarned that because the GSD is an excessively vocal dog, this technique may or may not work. But it is certainly worth a try in the instance that your dog is over-the-top vocal.

Method 1
- **Step 1:** Set up a situation in which you know he will bark but the stimulus is not so great that he won't be quiet quickly.
- **Step 2:** When he stops barking, reward him.
- **Step 3:** Link the verbal command, *"Quiet!"* with being quiet. Practice.

Method 2
- **Step 1:** Set up a situation in which you know he will bark but the stimulus is not so great that he won't be quiet quickly.
- **Step 2:** Use a slight, quick, and light leash tug that is just enough to momentarily distract him from barking, and instantly say *"Quiet!"* in a *low, calm* voice, and reward— all before he starts barking again.
- **Step 3:** Keep practicing until he responds quickly with silence.

Bolting

Dealing with a full-size, adult GSD that has gotten into the habit of bolting by you to get out the front door is no fun. If he's bolting, he will take every opportunity for "freedom" that he can get. He will bolt through an

Bolting as a Dominant Behavior?

Bolting is a dangerous habit to develop. Not only could your GSD become injured or lost, but pushing his way past you through doorways is obnoxious and could lead to more serious behavior issues. Initially, bolting could just be a sign of impulsiveness or wanting to get out to run. If you allow your dog to constantly push everyone out of the way to be "first" through doorways, you are "shaping" a dominant behavior. If you allow this shaping to continue, and if you have a dog that would like to live by his rules, he will interpret the "first through the door" as you're okay with him making the rules. You do not want this to happen, so whether it's for dominance or just because your GSD is a bit wild, make sure to train him not to bolt. Obedience training helps to establish your leadership in an effective but non-confrontational way. Be sure to work on the *wait* command, as this will help with open doorways, gates, etc.

open gate when you are trying to take out the trash, knocking you over in the process. Or, he may bolt when you open the truck door when you're at the park, before you can get a leash on him. Bolting is not only annoying, but it can also create a dangerous loose dog situation.

Teaching *Wait*

Method
- **Step 1:** Put him on leash.
- **Step 2:** With your GSD at your side, start to open the door.
- **Step 3:** When he starts to lunge forward, give him a light, quick tug on the leash (just enough to stop him) and shut the door.

Note: Again, the tug is not a harsh snap of the leash, it is not wheeling the dog around, it is not even a rough leash correction. It is like a tap on the shoulder to say, "Hey, stop." Remember, you're trying to teach him something. You're not punishing him.

- **Step 4:** Continue to do this until he stands or sits and does not try to run out the door. Reward him when he is good.
- **Step 5:** Make the exercise harder by keeping the door open longer. Follow the same steps as 1–4 but incrementally keep the door open longer each time. Reward him when he is good. If he breaks his *sit*, back up to less time with the door open and use a light leash correction if necessary.

Teaching *Get Back*

Method
- **Step 1:** Find a location in your home that has a definite boundary, such as a doorway or a change in the type of flooring (e.g., wood floor to carpet or tile floor to carpet). With your dog in the doorway, turn toward him.
- **Step 2:** While facing him, shuffle your feet forward and walk into him.
- **Step 3:** Tell him, "*Back!*" as he backs up.

  Note: If your GSD tries to push past you to go through the barrier first, perform the exercise with him on leash.
- **Step 4:** Release with an "*OK!*" Reward and praise him for backing up.
- **Step 5:** Keep practicing so that all you need to say is "*Back up!*" and your GSD immediately starts backing up.

Counter Surfing

The GSD could quite possibly be the king (or queen) of counter surfing. With his athleticism, he can easily jump on kitchen counters or the dining room table and effortlessly remove a cooling roast or a thawing chicken. He is adept, too, at sniffing out miniscule amounts of anything that is remotely edible. Simply put, the GSD can inspect your counter and all its goods at any time.

Trash Can Bandits

GSDs are adroit at breaking into virtually any "dog proof" trash can.

Solution: Lock the trash can behind cabinet doors or crate your dog when you aren't home.

The greatest problem with counter surfing is he won't do it when you're watching.

There are two methods that are 100 percent successful in stopping counter surfing, and both are *easy* to do.

1. Crate your GSD when you aren't home.
2. Do not leave food on the counter.

If you insist on leaving food out and not crating your dog, or if your dog is so bold that he tries to counter surf *in your presence*, try the following.

Method 1: Tether your GSD to your belt when working in the kitchen. If he attempts to take food off the counter, use a quick leash pop and a *low-voiced* "Ah, Ah!"

Method 2: You will need a corner mirror for this method. If you know your GSD will check out the counter as soon as you are not in the room, leave the room but remain just around the corner. Using the corner mirror, watch your dog. The second he jumps up to check out the counter, immediately come around the corner and say "Ah, Ah!" in a low voice.

Method 3: If you are not in the home, stack plastic cups on the counter. When he reaches up to the counter, the cups come tumbling down, hopefully deterring your dog from jumping again.

Note: Your GSD could decide to eat the cups, causing sharp edges to be ingested, and a more serious medical emergency to occur.

Method 4: If you are not in the home and your dog is incorrigible—consider a "scat" mat. The mat has a slight, electrical charge and is often used with cats to keep them off counters.

Note 1: Your GSD could try to chew the mat once he's pulled it off the counter.

Note 2: Your GSD could be willing to suffer the slight shock to get the food he wants.

Destructive Chewing

A GSD that is no longer teething but still chews on everything is usually an unsupervised, bored dog. Your first step is to make sure that he has more exercise than you think he needs and that you mentally challenge him throughout the day. A tired, mentally satisfied GSD is a good dog.

If your GSD's physical and mental needs are being met, and he is still destructively chewing shoes, furniture, toys (not his), doors, drywall, etc., try these methods.

Method 1: Give him appropriate chews, such as stuffed and frozen Kongs, Nylabones, or other hard, dense rubber toys that are not easily destroyed and that cannot be swallowed.

Method 2: See your veterinarian. If the source of your GSD's chewing and destruction is anxiety based—and he is getting exercise and tons of training—he could benefit from medical intervention.

Digging

The German Shepherd Dog is an excellent digger. With a minimum of effort, he can dig a small crater in your backyard or a tunnel under the fence to freedom. When addressing a digging dog, the first question you need to answer is why is he digging?

Is he digging because he's bored? Your GSD might start digging if he hasn't had enough mental and physical stimulation. You'll need to interact with him more, exercise him more, and train him more. And, you will need to make sure you never leave him unattended in the backyard. You might also consider making a digging pit. Create a sand box for your GSD and bury some of his favorite things for him to find and dig out. Make sure you clean him off before he comes back in the house.

Is he digging because of something in your yard? If your yard is host to moles or voles, he could be digging with a purpose. Of course, he could dig up your entire yard before he personally eradicates the yard of these burrowing creatures, but he will do the job. You just may not like his heavy landscaping approach.

Is he digging because he is hot? Dogs will dig shallow pits to reach cooler ground to lie on. If he's digging to cool down, make sure he is not left outside on hot days and provide a cooling mat (available in pet supply stores) to help him regulate his body temperature.

Is he digging because he is trying to escape? This last reason could be boredom but more likely it is hormones, as intact males (and intact females in season) will and do find ways to escape backyards. If your GSD has not been altered and you are having difficulties keeping him in your yard even with plenty of physical and mental stimulation, consider neutering him immediately. This should remove "wanderlust" from the digging equation.

Fence Jumping

If a GSD wants to escape a six-foot privacy fence, he can do it. If your GSD is jumping over your fence, your first step in solving the problem is to figure out why he is trying to escape.

Is he intact? An intact male GSD will scent a female in season within a mile, which is all the reason he needs to escape and take off. Likewise, if you have a female in season, in addition to having all the boys try to get in your yard, at some point your female will be desperate enough to try to escape your yard. Neuter or spay your GSD.

Is he bored? Exercise and lots of training will help keep your GSD in his backyard.

If you've taken care of the above possible fence-jumping issues, con-

sider these fencing modifications to make it more difficult for your dog to scale the fence.

Change the fencing. GSDs can use a chain-link fence as if it was a ladder. If you install a 6', solid wood privacy fence, he will not have any footing.

Add height. Add a 12- or 18-inch addition to the top of the fence and make sure it slants inward. The inward slant makes it exceptionally difficult for the dog to go over the fence.

Install Coyote Rollers. Coyote Rollers are rolling pvc pipes mounted at the top of a fence. Designed to keep coyotes *out* of a yard, these rollers also keep a jumping GSD *in* the

yard. With nothing to grip at the top of the fence to pull his body over, the GSD can't get over the fence.

Add an invisible fence. The invisible fence is a system in which a line with an electric charge is buried along the perimeter of the property. The dog wears a collar that begins to buzz him when he is approaching the buried electric cable or "invisible" fence. An invisible fence does not work as an effective fence on its own. If a GSD wants to get to the other side of an invisible fence, he will bear the pain of the electric shock to get out of the yard, but he won't bear the pain of the shock to return to his yard. Additionally, an invisible fence as the sole barrier to a yard does not keep other animals and people from coming into the unfenced yard.

Note: Where an invisible fence can be helpful, however, is in conjunction with an existing, solid fence. The combination of an electric, invisible fence and a solid, 6-foot privacy fence could be enough to deter the escaping GSD. **Note:** Invisible fences are not cheap and if it doesn't work, it could be an expensive "test."

Consider an electric, solor-powered fence. Finally, you can consider putting an electric fence at the top of a fence that is powered by a solar panel. Caution needs to be taken in that the charge from the fence must not be so strong as to injure the dog, and it cannot be so limited as to not be a deterrent to the fence-jumping dog.

Jumping Up

When your GSD is a little puppy, he will jump up to give you kisses and to get attention and pats. The act of jumping up is a friendly behavior. So, to prevent your GSD from getting in the habit of jumping on people as a friendly hello (which is not fun when he's full grown), there are several things you can do.

Method 1: When the GSD is jumping up on people. Teach him the *sit* to greet people. When he realizes that he must be sitting to receive pats and treats, it doesn't take too long for the little guy to slam his rear-end to the floor in anticipation of receiving treats. Adolescent and rescue GSDs can be taught this, too. If the full-grown GSD is in the habit of jumping up on people, be ready for this behavior. Have him on a leash and set up a situation in which you know he will jump up (e.g., your spouse walking into the house). Have a loose leash on your GSD, but make the loop short so that when he jumps up he cannot jump on the person. Then, when your GSD jumps up, keep your hand low so he cannot gain height when he is jumping and he immediately hits the end of the leash. Put him immediately in a *sit.* He can be rewarded for the *sit.* Practice this until he is no longer jumping up on people

Method 2: When the GSD is jumping up on you. If he is not on a leash (and you haven't yet trained a solid *sit* command), then do this: When he jumps up toward you, raise

What Not to Do with the GSD that Is Jumping Up

Do not pull back hard on the leash. Pulling hard on the leash makes the GSD physically rear up in an aggressive position. It is true that the GSD's original intent was not one of aggression but one of a friendly greeting. However, by putting your GSD in an aggressive position, you are creating an aggressive greeting. You are literally positioning him to aggressively confront people instead of being friendly.

your knee so that rather than him hitting you with his front paws, his chest hits your knee and throws him a bit off balance, which stops the jump. (**Note:** this is *not* kneeing the dog aggressively or with malice. This is simply putting a barrier between you and the jumping dog. He hits your knee; you do not—under any circumstances—knee the dog.) Then, put him in a *sit.* Reward him when he is providing a good *sit.* And, work on that *sit* so he will put his haunches to the ground rather than jump and knock you over.

Self-Mutilation

GSDs have a higher propensity for self-mutilation than most breeds. Self-mutilation typically includes either tail chewing or limb chewing. Once a dog begins self-mutilation, it is very hard to reverse the situation.

Self-mutilation is generally seen in dogs that suffer from high levels of anxiety. It can also be seen in high-drive, high-energy dogs that are over-crated; however, it can also be observed in GSDs that simply do not have enough activity or mental stimulation.

If you suspect that your GSD is having anxiety issues, take him to a qualified GSD trainer/handler. A GSD expert can help determine if the cause of the self-mutilation is from a lack of mental and physical stimulation or if it is something else.

If the GSD's situation cannot be improved through increased mental and physical stimulation, then consult with a veterinarian.

Note: A veterinary consult is needed if the dog has begun self-mutilation, as secondary infections and other medical issues will arise very quickly.

Chapter Eleven
Aggression

Aggression in dogs can take many forms. In fact, there are 23 known types of aggression, including dog-dog aggression, fear aggression, possessive aggression, territorial aggression, resource guarding, dominance, etc. Most dogs with aggression issues do not have just one form of aggression; rather, they have multiple forms of aggression. However, 90 percent of aggression issues stem from a dog's fear of something or someone.

A full-grown GSD with aggression issues is difficult for the experienced GSD owner to handle and can be terrifying for the novice owner. Once a dog has bitten someone, regardless of the reason for the bite, the dog is not considered placeable by any reputable shelter or GSD rescue. So, if the dog is given up for adoption, he will be euthanized.

How does an adorable, fluffy little GSD grow up to be a snarling, lunging, frightening adult dog?

Many types of aggression do not begin to show up until a GSD begins to sexually mature, around six to seven months of age. Most forms of aggression can be avoided almost completely if the GSD has been well socialized with both dogs and people since he was born. Dominance and territorial aggression, along with other types, can be lessened in some dogs driven by hormones through neutering.

Occasionally, a novice owner may think that their GSD is aggressive, when he is actually showing submissive behaviors, such as "smiling." Smiling is an odd-looking behavior in which the dog is showing his teeth; however, his entire body language is one of friendliness. His teeth are not bared aggressively, for example, with his nose curled up, eyes narrowed, and with aggressive, red-light posturing. Smiling is not aggressive; it is a friendly, submissive gesture.

Or, an inexperienced GSD owner may think his or her GSD is "biting," when in fact the GSD is exhibiting herding nips, which are not meant to injure the child or family member. Herding nips, which are controlled and do not break the skin, are used by the GSD to round up his flock, which in the home would translate into herding children into one room or to a corner in the yard. Safety pulls are another herding behavior. Safety pulls are used by a GSD when he senses that a member of his flock is in imminent danger. He grabs a limb of the animal and pulls it to safety. Safety pulls *can* break the skin because the dog increases his hold if the livestock in need of rescuing struggles to get away. A safety pull on a child would hurt. Herding nips and holds are not acceptable behavior in the home; however, they are different than a fear bite or a bite to exert dominance in that the herding based nips/holds are never intended to hurt or injure the flock member.

So, how do you know if your dog is really behaving aggressively or if it's something else? Know your GSD's body language. Refer to pages 49–56 for descriptions and images of green-, yellow-, and red-light behaviors. Also, read through the different types of aggression described below and familiarize yourself with behaviors that are linked to the different types of aggression, as well as how to be proactive and prevent aggressive behaviors from developing.

As always, if you feel uncertain as to a dog's behaviors, consult with an experienced GSD trainer immediately. Much heartache can be averted if issues are nipped in the bud before they become serious problems. Aggression issues can manifest quickly if the initial issue is not handled swiftly. Appropriate handling and consistent corrective training will be necessary to resolve an aggression issue.

If a dog is showing red-light behaviors *at any age*, the best avenue is to take the dog to a skilled and experienced GSD trainer/handler for an unbiased evaluation and a plan of action.

Owner-Directed or Dominance Aggression

This form of aggression is more commonly seen in GSDs that are either living in a home with no rules (in which they have taken it upon themselves to make the rules) or GSDs that have a genetic propensity to be dominant.

Signs: Pushing through doorways before the owner, red-light behaviors when asked to move off a couch or bed, posturing stiffly, reactive to commands, or ignores commands completely.

Preventive Measures: Training—continuously and consistently from the time the GSD is a small puppy. Obeying commands and having house rules will ensure the even-tempered GSD knows his place in the family. Training also helps the GSD that is genetically predisposed to seek the leadership role to maintain a second-in-command position without direct confrontation. Neutering before the GSD reaches sexual maturity is essential for the genetically predisposed dominant GSD.

Fear Aggression

Fear aggression is the most common form of aggression and not surprisingly is the most common source for bites. Fear aggression is found primarily in dogs that lack socialization and/or have a real fear or terror of a type of person (or all people), other dogs (or specific breeds—usually from a past experience), or things, such as the garbage truck.

Signs: The dog will show yellow-light fear behaviors that will escalate into red-light fear behaviors. When the source of the fear becomes too close and the GSD has no means of flight, he will choose fight.

Preventive Measures: Socialize as much as possible, avoiding yellow-light behavior reactions to people, dogs, or things. Reward good behavior and never comfort transitory or red-light behaviors. This type of aggression can be avoided and/or modified with good socialization training. Habituation or acclimation to scary things (trash cans, ceiling fans, vacuum cleaners, etc.) is also important to prevent yellow-light behaviors from escalating to red-light behaviors.

Territorial/ Protective Aggression

Many owners purchase GSDs with the thought that they will make

their family pet into a combination family pet and guard dog. A dog that is trained for guard dog work does not make a good pet. A GSD that is well socialized, well trained, and likes people will make the best dog for protection because this GSD can determine a good, friendly person from one with ill intents. The family pet, however, should never be *trained* to guard against *everyone*. This makes for a very volatile situation, as everyone who enters the home, including your mother or your children's friends, are targets.

Signs: A GSD can become territorial of his home and property, usually to the fence line and extending beyond. GSDs can become territorial/protective aggressive of children and family members in the home, too. The territorial/protective aggressive dog can be territorial over certain high-value pieces of furniture in your home. Also, the GSD can become territorial/protective aggressive of *you*, his owner. If you are a timid or easily frightened person by nature, your sensitive GSD will pick up on your fearfulness and begin looking for the cause of your anxiety. From this point, even the friendliest of GSDs can become protective aggressive of his owner.

Preventive Measures: Walking and training your GSD away from your home—broadening his horizons—will help keep a GSD from becoming hyper-territorial of his home and yard. Continuous positive socialization in the home helps the GSD understand that kind people coming into his home is a good thing, too. Supervise all children at all times when your GSD is with them, and if you can't supervise directly, actively, and in near proximity, then separate the children from the dog.

Neuter your male dog. Neutering will help to lessen territorial tendencies in male dogs. If done early enough, it will also prevent the dog from getting in the habit of marking his territory with urine.

Teaching the *off* command (page 109) before you have a territorial/protective issue will allow you to tell a GSD to get off a high-value chair, couch, or bed without confrontation. Additionally, not allowing the GSD on the bed at any time will help keep the territorial aggressive dog from becoming protective of those common places. (**Note:** red-light behaviors on a coveted chair or bed may also be owner/dominant aggression, or a combination of owner/dominant and territorial/protective aggression.)

And, finally, if you *know* you are an anxious individual, keep a bit of slack in the leash so your dog does not pick up on your timidity. Or, have someone else in your family who is bold and outgoing by nature walk your dog or accompany you on your walks.

Three Types of Dog-on-Dog Aggression

Often, dog-on-dog aggression is lumped together as "dog aggressive." However, there are nuances that distinguish three types of dog aggression.

Related to Dominance

This type of dog-on-dog aggression can be seen at dog runs where groups of dogs are playing. The dog with dog-on-dog aggression that is related to dominance will overtly display pushy behaviors that show dominance to other dogs. These behaviors include putting a paw on the back of another dog, going nose-to-nose for a greeting instead of curling in a c-shape or offering a rear end to sniff, aggressively chasing another dog, and mounting other dogs. Dominance-related dog-on-dog aggression frequently ends with a dog fight with injuries.

Preventive Measures: Supervise all dog interactions with your GSD, being careful to remove your dog from a play situation in which he appears to become increasingly agitated or aroused. Not all GSDs are suited for large playgroups, dog parks, or doggie daycares. If this is the case, accept this trait and work on ensuring, through training, that he is tolerant on leash around other dogs.

Related to Pack (Siblings)

This type of dog-on-dog aggression is limited to the GSD's pack or immediate "family" of dogs. For example, if you have a home with four dogs, if one dog shows dog aggressive posturing and red-light behaviors, this is considered pack/sibling aggression. Owning a dog that is aggressive to other dogs in the home is a highly challenging situation. Puppies typically fold into a family pack of dogs with no issues. If the resident adult dog wants to be left alone, he makes his desire quickly understood and the puppy respects that. If the adult dog enjoys puppies, the pup continues to learn how to behave around other dogs, as he has a gentle and kind adult

teaching him dog play rules. On occasion, an adult dog will not be satisfied with telling the puppy to stay away from him; rather, the adult dog's interactions with the puppy may escalate to red-light aggressive behaviors, which could seriously injure or cause deadly injuries to the puppy. Similarly, the puppy may begin challenging the resident older dog when he, the puppy, begins to reach sexual maturity. As

the younger, stronger dog, if the adolescent GSD crosses into red-light behaviors with the resident dog, the adolescent GSD could seriously injure the adult dog. The potential for injury is high if the dogs are equally sized; if the other dogs in the home are small, the potential for deadly injuries is even greater.

Preventive Measures: How you introduce the new puppy or adult dog to current dogs in the home is important. Do not rush introductions, and be patient. Always work for positive interactions with no yellow-light behaviors.

- **Step 1:** Introduce the resident dog to the new puppy or dog on neutral territory using the dog socialization methods described on pages 62–64. Make sure that the resident dog and the new dog are amicable while walking and neither dog is exhibiting yellow-light behaviors. Green is go.
- **Step 2:** Keep the new puppy or dog safely separated from the other dog with a sturdy gate. With a puppy, put up a gate in a doorway to a room and set up the puppy in a crate in an x-pen. (**Tip:** Purchase a tall gate that is not easily scaled, or stack two gates, one above the other.) Allow the adult dog to observe the new puppy from the gate. The resident dog will be excited and may show some yellow-light behaviors; if he does, take him away from the gate and reward him for calm, relaxed behaviors.

- **Step 3:** Make sure to keep the resident dog active with plenty of exercise, continued training, and chews while he is in his crate. Your goal with the resident dog is to make him feel as if the arrival of the new dog brought him more attention, more toys, more walks, more playtime, etc. Dogs do not get jealous per se but they are aware if a new dog gets a treat and they don't or if the new dog gets a walk and they don't.
- **Step 4:** Continue to take multiple walks with the resident dog and the new GSD multiple times a day, with another person handling the resident dog, and then switching and handling the new GSD. If yellow-light behaviors are presented, move the dogs farther apart or one in front of the other and farther apart. Continue to reward good behaviors and calm yellow-light behaviors with distance.
- **Step 5:** Continue working to introduce the resident dog and the new GSD. Take it slowly, and remember it could be weeks before both dogs are comfortable enough to be in the same room without gates, x-pens, and crates to separate them. Even when the dogs appear to be all getting along, *never leave them together in the home without direct, close supervision*. Crate every dog when you leave the home.

Related to Fear

The dog with dog-on-dog aggression related to fear is acting out of fear for his life; it is "aggression" because the dog has chosen "fight" instead of "flight."

Dog-on-dog aggression related to fear can be dog specific (i.e., the dog behaves aggressively around one particular dog), toward dogs in general (i.e., the dog behaves this way with every dog he meets), or toward specific breeds (i.e., the dog behaves this way only around certain breeds).

Aggression related to fear appears at the red-light level much in the same way as dominance aggression; however, there are distinct differences that will help you determine why the dog is showing yellow-light and red-light behaviors related to fear. For a more in-depth discussion on fear and aggression, and the behaviors that distinguish fear from dominance, see Green-, Yellow-, and Red-Light Behaviors, pages 49–56.

Preventive Measures: Socializing a dog from the moment you have him as a puppy—or continuing the socialization of an adopted dog and ensuring that he has no negative experiences—will go far in preventing fear-related dog aggression. It is critically important, too, that you recognize bullying and/or aggressive behaviors in *other* dogs and do not allow these dogs to have contact with your dog. If you have a timid or fearful dog, follow the socialization guidelines for timid GSDs on pages 59–60 and 61–62.

Chase/Predatory Aggression

The progenitors of today's domestic dog lived by eating what they killed. As a pack, the domestic dog's ancestors would chase down an older, younger, or injured animal as game. The predation sequence is *see-chase-grab-kill*. In the vast majority of dogs, the predation sequence has been diluted but not totally eliminated. The act of chasing a ball reflects the domestic dogs' continued prey/play drive. Here it is noted as prey/play because the *see-chase-grab* part of the sequence is very much alive; however, the *kill* aspect is not part of the prey/play equation. Certain breeds, such as those from the herding group like the German Shepherd Dog, have a high-chase drive but the grab-bite part of the sequence is not present as often, as herding breeds are not intended to injure the livestock they are chasing. Dogs from other breed groups, such as those from the terrier group, have a high drive to *see-chase-grab-kill*.

In all breeds of dogs, movement is what begins the sequence of predation; how far your GSD will take the sequence is something that is instinctive and not something that is acquired. What your dog considers "prey" is where the issues begin. For example, though you might find it distasteful, your dog could run down squirrels, rabbits, and small birds. When this drive turns toward running down cats, it is a problem for owners who have cats; in fact, if a dog thinks that cats are prey, it is not possible to have the two species in the home together.

What if a dog has a predatory drive with smaller dogs? He cannot be around small dogs *ever*. Although you may be able to make him mind with heeling and *sits*, the instant he is not under your command control, he will go after a small dog the moment the small dog moves.

Preventive Measures: As noted above, chase/predatory aggression cannot be trained out of a dog, or modified. The only way for this dog to be safe around smaller animals and dogs is not to be around other animals and dogs.

Note: Chase/predatory aggression toward small animals is not the same as aggression toward small children and babies (see page 135). Whlie the two types of predation *could* be combined, this is not common.

Possessive Aggression

This type of aggression is typically seen when a dog has an item that is of high value (in his mind) and the dog does not want anyone or anything to come near him in the chance that they might try to take it away. Sometimes possessive aggression is directed only toward other dogs in his pack, in which case, the dogs generally understand that they are not to take his ball or toy away and nothing more comes of it. However, more often the possessive aggression that causes problems in a home is when the GSD has a high-value item and is willing to growl, snarl, snap, and bite if anyone tries to take it away from him. A distinct yellow-light behavior of a resource guarding dog is to lie down and tuck the item he does not want to give up under his chin. Note that the dog could be possessive aggressive with all his toys and chews but sometimes he is only possessive aggressive with *one* item, such as a favorite toy or an empty toilet paper roll that he stole from the bathroom.

of the dog's mouth *ever*. This is a tough one to teach children, as it is human nature to try to grab back a stolen toy, shoe, or doll, but it is an important skill to teach because it could save them from a serious bite. Additionally, if the GSD is resource guarding a particular item, never give him that item again. Or, if he likes to steal toilet paper rolls and then guard them, for example, keep the door to the bathroom shut at all times. See pages 112–113 for additional tips in safely separating a dog from the item he is guarding.

Aggression Toward Babies or Children

This form of aggression is dangerous. A dog with aggression toward babies or children is exceptionally unsafe and should not be in the home with newborns or young children.

Note: This form of aggression could also extend to a frail or mobility-compromised adult, such as an elderly family member. Dogs with this form of aggression are triggered by the crying noises of babies and young children, as well as the jerking, erratic movements of a child learning to walk. Dogs may be seen staring intensely at a child or baby, coupled with stiff, bristling body language. Make no mistake; this is *not* a mild "interest" in the child.

Aggression toward babies and children is often fear based, but it

Preventive Measures: Much of possessive aggression (sometimes called "resource guarding") is believed to be genetically based—or the propensity of the puppy developing possessive aggression is set in his genes. Regardless, there are steps you can take to be proactive and to prevent possessive aggression from occurring. There are also steps you can take to minimize the possessive aggressive behaviors shown by your dog, so you can create a safer environment in the family home.

Teach the *out* command (page 112): This exercise will allow you to retrieve an item the GSD may think is guard-worthy and is of high value in his mind. Also, and this is key, teach your children not to take things out

can be found in combination with territorial aggression, resource guarding, and chase/predatory aggression.

Preventive Measures: Introduce the young, malleable GSD puppy to the sounds of newborns and toddlers, as well as to the erratic movements of toddlers. Make sure all interactions are positive, and keep the puppy at a distance at which he feels safe and is exhibiting green-light behaviors, allowing a toddler to give him a treat, *but do not let the toddler poke, pull, or tug on the puppy!* Take the puppy regularly to a children's park to observe the sights and sounds of children playing, and reward green-light, relaxed behaviors. Quickly move the puppy farther away from the children if he shows yellow-light behaviors.

Remember, this is *prevention.* Never try to socialize a dog that shows even the slightest proclivity in attacking a baby or a small child.

Allow one child at a time to come up to offer your friendly, outgoing puppy a treat. Remember, you must be in complete control of interactions with children at all times. You cannot allow hugging, faces in the puppy's face, or any other behavior that would frighten the puppy or make him anxious. These are to be completely positive experiences only.

Critical: This bears repeating . . . If your GSD is aggressive toward babies and/or children, *do not risk your family members in an attempt to "rehab" the dog.* This is *not* a condition that can be "controlled" by an electric collar or by brutally training it out of a dog. The dog that truly has this form of aggression will continue to seek his opportunity until something tragic happens.

Redirected Aggression, Frustration-Elicited Aggression, and Barrier Aggression

These three types of aggressions are often intertwined. In other words, a dog may exhibit two or more of these types of aggression in the same incident. Breaking the specific types of aggression by examples is as follows.

Redirected aggression is the redirection of a tension or argument between two dogs to a third person or dog. A classic example of redirected aggression is when two dogs are fighting each other and you reach in to pull your dog back by his collar—and he bites *you.* Or, two dogs could be having a tense stand-off moment in the dog park when a third, happy-go-lucky dog comes along to investigate. In this scenario, redirected aggression can occur when one of the original dogs from the stand-off whips around and bites the happy-go-lucky dog.

Frustration aggression is when a dog acts aggressively out of frustration. For example, the dog is running up and down the fence line with another dog, barking and growling at what is on the other side of the fence. Suddenly, he turns and bites the dog he is running with along the fence line. This is considered frustration-elicited aggression, as the GSD wants to see what's on the other side of the fence and is frustrated when he can't. Or, you may be walking your GSD and he sees dogs playing in the park and really, really wants to go join them. So, he starts barking and lunging and leaping on his leash because of his frustration that he is being held back.

Barrier aggression can be seen in shelters and is generally described as a dog showing aggressive behaviors when a barrier, such as a fence, pen, window, kennel, etc., generates an elevated level of stress to the dog.

Preventive Measures: Exercise and mentally stimulate your GSD. Do not allow him in the backyard alone to even begin developing a barrier frustration. Work on socialization skills with your puppy from the beginning and if he isn't social with other dogs, work with him to be tolerant. If you know your dog will bite the other dog while running the fence, or when the delivery man comes to the door, then prevent these situations from happening. Do not allow your dog access to the front door where he can work himself up into a tizzy over the delivery man and his box. Excitement often turns into arousal, which is a step away from aggression.

Food-Related Aggression

Often, food-related aggression, in which the dog is aggressive toward anyone or any dog that comes near his food, is considered to be the result of the dog's environment. Food-related aggression often occurs when a dog has experienced an abusive situation or has come from a multiple dog "home" in which the owner threw a bag of dog food out to a pack of dogs either out of ignorance or to *encourage* the dogs to fight with each other. Regardless of the cause for the aggression, the GSD with food-related aggression has learned to fight for his food as a matter of survival.

A food-related aggressive dog is dangerous. Since his aggression is survival based, he *will* fight for his food, and is therefore not safe around children or other dogs. This is a type of aggression that can be worked with; however, it is a reward-based training process in which the dog is taught the *leave it* command when he sees or walks by food. He is also rewarded when he allows food to be taken away from him. The fight for self-preservation is so strong that this is not training that should be undertaken by a pet owner.

Preventive Measures: The best prevention for food-related aggression is to never let your GSD feel he has to fight for his food. Feeding one of his meals each day by hand reinforces that the food comes from you and that you are giving him food.

You can also practice "adding" to the GSD puppy's food by hand so that he is used to good things happening when a hand approaches his bowl. Acclimate your GSD to having hands near his food when he is young and has not begun to develop resource guarding traits. The result of this training is to condition the dog to hand + food bowl = extra good treat. For this exercise, you will need a small handful of high-value treats. Every time you feed your puppy, put him in a *sit* to wait for his food, release him to eat his food, then reach into his bowl several times while he is eating, and drop a high-value treat in with his kibble. Continue until your handful of treats is gone.

Note: If he is already showing yellow-light behaviors around his food, do *not* attempt to do this exercise. Also, never remove food from the dog's bowl; only add food. The purpose is to connect a hand approaching his bowl with good things.

Play Aggression

A dog with play aggression is the dog that cannot play well with other dogs. He is the dog that can't self-regulate and calm himself down during play. He is the dog that may start off playing hard but works himself up until he is so agitated that playing ends up in a squabble or even a dog fight. (Dogs that play well will often be seen leaving the play group and lying down away from the dogs that don't, almost as if they are in a calming, time-out.)

Preventive Measures: Unlike "Social Aggression" (see below) in which proper early socialization skills learned with littermates and positive early interactions with kind, adult dogs can minimize awkward social behavior (that sparks aggression), play aggression is the dog that simply can't play without becoming increasingly agitated until excitement escalates to aggression.

As for prevention, there's not much you can do other than not allow your dog to play with others. If your play-aggressive GSD is terrible with other dogs but he's great with every person he's ever met, focus your training efforts on making your GSD tolerant and non-reactive of other dogs when he is on leash.

Social Aggression

A dog with social aggression is the dog that is socially awkward with other dogs. Somewhere along the line the social aggressive dog didn't learn the right socialization skills or body language to behave correctly in situations where there are a number of dogs present. Perhaps he was taken away from his littermates to soon, or maybe he didn't have a kind, adult dog to show him the ropes. Sometimes, a dog with social aggression may play well with one particular dog or maybe even two dogs, but being in a large group of

dogs seems to overstimulate him. Social aggression can also stem from a bad experience with a large group of dogs, such as at a doggie daycare (that is not carefully supervised).

Preventive Measures: Puppies need to stay with their littermates and mother for at least eight weeks, preferably nine weeks or even more, to learn proper social behaviors with other dogs. Continued socializing of the young GSD should include a kind, adult dog that will tell the pup when he is playing nicely and put the young pup in his place when he's not playing nicely. Avoid situations, such as large dog parks or unsupervised doggie day cares, as this will prevent negative experiences from creating a socially aggressive dog.

Medically Based Aggressions

The following forms of aggression are not inherited or the result of negative experiences. Rather, these aggressions are those with a medical or health-based source that can only be treated by a veterinarian. Descriptions of these aggressions follow; however, with all of these forms of aggression, if your GSD has had a long history of being friendly, gentle, and well socialized, and suddenly he is exhibiting red-light, aggressive behaviors, the cause could very well be medically related. Your first call should be to secure an appointment with your veterinarian.

Maternal Aggression

Maternal aggression, in which a female dog attacks her own newborn puppies, is believed to be caused by a change in hormones, and is seen infrequently but only in dogs that have just given birth to a litter of puppies. This form of aggression can be successfully treated medically but requires an immediate consult with the veterinarian so as not to endanger the newly born puppies.

Health-Related Aggression (General)

If your GSD has had no previous episodes of aggression and suddenly he is avoiding other dogs, reacting to being touched, unwilling to play, or exhibiting nighttime aggression, consult with your veterinarian immediately. Numerous diseases can cause odd, aggressive behaviors.

Seizure-Related Aggression

Researchers have been studying the behavioral changes in dogs suffering from idiopathic epilepsy. These changes include an increase in fear, anxiety, defensive aggression, and abnormal perception. If your dog is suffering from seizures and is exhibiting heightened aggressive behaviors, discuss this change immediately with your veterinarian.

Aggression Influenced by Medications

With every medication, there is a balance between the severities of the side effects versus the benefit of taking the medication. Medications that may contribute to aggression in dogs include prednisone, phenobarbital, and corticosteroids. If you suspect that a medication could be causing your dog to show aggressive behaviors, consult with your veterinarian immediately.

Pain Aggression

Pain has been known to cause sudden outbreaks of aggression in dogs. Spinal pain may cause a dog to snap when someone tugs on a leash snapped to his collar. A painful ear infection may cause a dog to snarl when touched on the head. A dog suffering from untreated, chronic hip dysplasia could become aggressive when someone tries to move him.

Sex-Related Aggression

Sex-related aggression is typically, but not always, limited to male dogs. Dogs with this form of aggression will hump dogs of both sexes, as well as humans. This behavior often stems from lack of socialization with dogs, as well as a lack of rank and control in a pack situation.

Preventive Measures: Socialize your GSD with other dogs that display correct dog behaviors, are kind, and do not tolerate socially unacceptable behavior from puppies. These types of dogs will teach your pup to behave without harming him. Training your dog will help him to grow up understanding his place and rank in the family. Neutering (or spaying) the GSD that continues to exhibit sex-related aggression can help to diffuse the situation.

Hyperactive Aggression

Some dogs have an inability to focus, appearing nervous and constantly moving and/or panting.

Preventive Measures: If a dog is exhibiting an inability to focus along with hyperactive behaviors, talk to your veterinarian about your dog's diet. High protein diets are not good for a dog with hyperactive aggression; it is thought to be similar to giving mounds of sugar to a child who has inability to focus. A common theory is that a low protein diet, exercise, and a strict routine will help a dog with hyperactivity to regain focus.

Reactive Aggression

The GSD that is reactive aggressive is the dog that is barking, whining, lunging, and hypervigilant. He is super reactive to other dogs and spends his day as if he is expecting something dangerous to jump out at him from every shadow and every corner. Causes of reactive aggression include genetics, poor socialization with humans and dogs, hormones, and neurophysical disorders.

Preventive Measures: It is impossible to change a dog's genetics; however, you can work to create positive experiences when socializing this dog with people and dogs. Provide the dog with sufficient physical exercise and mental stimulation through training and mental activities, such as a puzzle toy that dispenses treats. Management of reactive aggression also includes removing opportunities for the GSD to be hypervigilant (block him from being able to watch people walk by the house or from watching the delivery man come to the door). Also, you can work with a skilled trainer to pinpoint other behavior issues that can be managed with good training strategies.

Chapter Twelve

Activities for Your German Shepherd Dog

The GSD is a very versatile dog and the world is his oyster when it comes to participating in competitive sports and non-competitive, titling, and certification events. Some programs are structured so that every GSD should participate, learn, and benefit from the training. Other programs, such as performance events and certain non-competitive activities, have physical and temperament requirements to be successful.

Non-Competitive Events and Programs

AKC S.T.A.R. Puppy Program

This program was designed by the American Kennel Club (AKC) to reward dog owners for getting their puppies off to a good training start. The S.T.A.R. program is designed to help new owners understand their puppies' behaviors, as well as to teach owners how to train their pups. The program also includes sharing practical skills for house-training, and how best to deal with typical puppy behaviors, such as chewing.

The S.T.A.R. program is taught by an AKC-approved Canine Good Citizen (CGC, see below) evaluator and is for puppies up to a year old. Once you and your puppy have completed the six-week course, the instructor will administer a test. Upon passing, you will receive a medal, as well an application to enroll in the AKC S.T.A.R. Puppy Program. As a member of the puppy program, you will receive a monthly email newsletter that includes training tips and other good puppy information.

For more information on the puppy program, go to the AKC website. To find an AKC S.T.A.R. puppy training program near you, go to *www.akc.org/dog-owners/training/akc-star-puppy.*

Canine Good Citizen (CGC)

The CGC was a test that was introduced by the AKC in 1989, but as of January 1, 2013, the CGC is an official AKC title. What this means is that if your GSD is registered with the AKC, and he passes the CGC test, for a minimal processing fee your dog will have the suffix "CGC" attached to his name in the AKC registry.

One of the biggest reasons to train your GSD with the intention of passing the CGC test is that this title is recognized by many home insurance companies, rental agencies, and military housing installations as certification that the GSD is not a homeowner's liability (i.e., not a dangerous dog). In addition, the CGC is a requirement for many certifying therapy organizations, if you are interested in working with your GSD in animal-assisted therapy.

There is no age limit for the CGC test, and puppies that have been fully vaccinated can participate, as well as dogs of any age. If you test your puppy and he passes, it is recommended that you and your GSD retake the test when he is an adult, as once dogs become sexually mature, they can also experience changes in their temperament and behavior—particularly if you do not stay on top of their socialization skills and training.

For those interested in taking the CGC test, it is advisable (but not required) to take a training class with an AKC-registered CGC evaluator. The skills that you and your dog will be tested on include accepting a friendly stranger; sitting politely for petting; appearance and grooming (the GSD must allow someone to check his ears and front feet, simulating a groomer or a veterinarian); walking on a loose leash; walking through a crowd (this part of the test demonstrates that the GSD is under control in crowded public places and is polite); *sit* and *down* on command; *stay* in place (you will be able to choose the position that your dog will be left in for a time period); recall (on leash from 10 feet); reaction to another dog (on leash, walking up to another handler and dog on leash); reaction to a distraction; and supervised separation (demonstrates that your GSD can be left with a trusted person and maintain calm and good manners while you go out of sight for three minutes).

Community Canine (Canine Good Citizen Advanced— CGCA)

This is a more advanced test than the CGC, as the test for the Community Canine title

is given in real-world situations, as opposed to a controlled area such as a training facility or a show ring. There is no age requirement for the CGCA; however, the dog must have achieved his CGC title first before testing for the CGCA.

The tests are performed on leash with the dog wearing a buckle collar, martingale collar (also called a "hound" collar—a collar that allows for some tightening of the broad, non-choking collar to prevent slender headed dogs from backing out of their collars and running off), or body harness. Special training collars, such as pinch collars or head collars, are not permitted. The handler may talk to his or her GSD and provide verbal praise throughout the test; however, no treats or toys are allowed.

The Community Canine test has ten components, and the dog must pass all ten to receive his title. The test includes: sitting, standing, or lying down peacefully while the dog handler sits at a table to fill out paperwork, share a snack, or talk to another person; walking on a loose leash in a natural area, such as a park, and making turns, stopping and changing pace; walking on a loose leash through a real crowd; walking past other leashed dogs without reacting or pulling; sitting at least 30 seconds while the owner stops to talk to at least three other people with dogs; allowing a person carrying a backpack, gym bag, computer bag, etc., to approach and pet him after placing the item on the ground; performing a *leave it* past food on the ground; performing a *down-stay* or *sit-stay* on a 20-foot line while the owner walks to pick something up and returns to the dog; performing a recall with distractions; remaining in a *sit-stay* or *stand-stay* while the owner leaves the room through a doorway or passageway, and then coming when called.

Urban Canine Good Citizen (CGCU)

The purpose of the Urban Canine Good Citizen is to test the skills of the dog in an urban setting in which there are cars, busy streets to cross, noises, and distractions. It is given in the "real" world and not in a training facility or show ring. It is possible to test for both the CGC and the CGCU on the same day, but the dog and owner must take and pass the CGC first before taking the CGCU test.

The CGCU test, as with the CGC and the CGCA, must be given by an AKC-registered CGC evaluator. The CGCU tests the dog in ten different scenarios: exiting and entering a doorway to a building without pulling; walking through a crowd on a busy urban sidewalk; reacting appropriately to a variety of noises, movements, and city surfaces (i.e., horns, sirens, skateboards, runners, concrete, grass, grates, etc.); crossing a busy street without pulling and standing or sitting on street corners while waiting to cross the street; ignoring food and trash on the sidewalk; allowing a person with a handbag, a little dog in a carrier, etc., to come up and pet him; walking under control in a building with a slick floor; performing a three-minute *down-stay* with owner as the owner stops in a lobby or outdoor area to have a snack; demonstrating that he can go up stairs and enter, ride, and exit an elevator; providing evidence that the he is housetrained for an apartment, condo, or city living (by observation of the dog during the test and with owner verification); showing proficiency to travel in a car (small dogs are allowed to show that they can ride in a carrier on the subway).

Non-Competitive Service Activities

Search and Rescue (SAR)

The German Shepherd Dog has a long history of involvement in search and rescue (SAR), beginning most notably with his service as a hospital dog in World War I, in which he searched for injured soldiers needing urgent medical care in war-torn fields, woods, and urban environments. His job then, of going back to his medic handler and bringing the medic back to the injured soldier, is similar to the manner in which he performs "live" searches today; except now the medic is a civilian volunteer dog handler and the GSD is searching for lost (and possibly injured) civilians.

In addition to live searches, today's SAR dogs can be trained to perform Human Remains Detection (HRD) on both land and on boats or on the shorelines of bodies of water. SAR dogs work in wilderness, as well as in rural, suburban, and urban settings. SAR dogs can search for a single person, or in the case of a natural disaster or mass casualty, they can look for many people. SAR dogs may also be trained to "trail," which is following a scent-specific trail rather than searching for *any* live person or an HRD search.

Preparing a GSD to work in SAR requires dedication and a lot of training. It takes approximately two years to certify a dog in SAR, and that is if all runs smoothly with the dog and handler's training. Most volunteer SAR handlers work full-time jobs during the week and devote their weekends to training their dogs. It can be hot or cold, raining or snowing and training continues. SAR dogs must be skilled in basic obedience and be standouts in tracking and scent work. To be successful, the SAR dog is typically *not* the dog that you would select as a pet. SAR dogs need to be exceptionally high-drive (think of the dog that is constantly searching for his ball and cannot rest unless he has it or you are throwing it). He must also have a sound structure and not suffer from hip or elbow dysplasia, as he will be required to work in rough terrain.

Don't forget the handler part of SAR. In addition to the countless hours of training every weekend, the handler must be fit and capable of dealing with the elements outdoors and traversing rugged terrain. He or she must also be trained in navigation, map use, crime scene preservation, as well as dog handling and training. Once certified and a working member of a SAR group, the handler must also have employment at which he is able to leave on short notice and assist in a search when called.

Good SAR training groups require outside testing sources and evaluations. Additional requirements for SAR handlers and their dogs may vary from state to state, so it is important to talk to state and local law enforcement, but most require handlers to have no felony records. Background checks of handlers are required by most states, too.

Therapy Dogs

Therapy Dog visits to children's hospitals, rehabilitation centers, and assisted-living facilities are becoming more and more common. Dogs, without question, can be uplifting visitors for patients, as well as for the medical staff that cares for the patients. Currently, there are two types of therapy work a dog can qualify for: animal-assisted activities in which dogs are used to improve morale and to cheer up patients, and animal-assisted therapy, when the dog is part of the patient's care plan.

Many German Shepherd Dogs are excellent therapy dogs; however, to be a therapy dog, the GSD must have a calm, laid-back, and nearly bomb-proof temperament. In addition, he must have a genuine love for people, be fine around other dogs, and be exceptionally well socialized. He cannot let small changes in his environment faze him, and he must be able to adapt calmly to all situations.

Most certifying therapy organizations require that the dog is at least a year old and has passed (at a minimum) the CGC test before they will test the dog with their own certifying obedience and behavioral testing.

Owners interested in pursuing therapy dog certification for their GSDs must not only socialize, train, and test their GSDs, but they also must be willing to regularly bathe their GSDs and keep their nails appropriately trimmed, as therapy dogs must be clean and free of as much shed hair as possible to be allowed to work and/or volunteer in therapy situations. Organizations that certify therapy dogs include

Therapy Dogs International, Therapy Dogs United, and R.E.A.D. (Reading Education Assistance Program).

Fun, Outdoor Activities

Swimming

The activity of swimming, whether in a lake, pond, bay, ocean, or the backyard pool, is great exercise for your GSD. Swimming is demanding exercise that is gentle on dogs with hip or elbow issues. A caveat to swimming as a great outlet for the GSD's sometimes boundless energy is that the GSD must enjoy water. Avoid introducing the GSD to ocean water on high surf days, as the sound alone can be intimidating to all but the bravest of German Shepherd Dogs. Instead, try to introduce your GSD on a "barely there" surf day or in a calmer body of water such as a sound, bay, or lake. Also, make sure the body of water has a gradual entryway and not a sudden drop off. If your GSD loves to retrieve, toss his ball (or another item that will float) a foot or two into the water to help get his toes wet.

When introducing your GSD to a pool, mark the pool step entry with red flags so that he knows exactly where to exit the pool. For his first time in the pool, use a properly fitted dog life jacket and ease him into the water. Be careful, as once he starts swimming, he could initially be a little

frantic and his toenails could rake your skin.

When your GSD swims in freshwater or saltwater, make sure to provide him with plenty of clean, fresh water to drink—either from your tap at home or from bottled water. Ingesting large amounts of salt water will cause the GSD to vomit; freshwater lakes and streams often contain *giardia* and other parasites and/or bacteria that could make your dog quite ill. Additionally, clean your dog's ears after swimming with an ear drying formula to help prevent fungal and/or bacterial infections.

Camping/Hiking

If you're an avid hiker or backpacker, or enjoy camping in remote (or semi-remote) areas, your GSD will enjoy the mental and physical stimulation that comes with every good outdoor activity. Although you will be in the heart of nature, your GSD must be good with people, as he will meet people on the trails; he must be good with other dogs, as he will meet other hikers and campers with dogs and he must be nonreactive; and your dog must have excellent command of his obedience training, so that you can immediately control him, halt him, recall him, etc., to avoid injury or interaction with dangerous wildlife. If you are planning on having your GSD carry some of the supplies for the hike, make sure his backpack is fitted by an expert in dog hiking equipment, and begin practicing (and gradually add-

ing weight to your dog's pack) with your GSD a few weeks before going on your hike. Make sure your initial hikes are easy, short trails that are easy on the paws, shaded, and have soft leaf or needle-covered paths.

Additionally, remember to pack water for your dog and carry bags to "pack out" poop on day hikes. On longer hikes and for overnight camping, make sure you've packed a foam pad for your dog to sleep on and a lightweight wool blanket in cold weather. Also, bring LED lights or glow stick bracelets to attach to your dog's collar so that you can see him in the dark. And, don't forget a first aid pack with bandages, anti-septic, liquid bandage, and tweezers for thorns and ticks. Additionally, make sure your dog has sufficient

flea and tick preventives for the great outdoors.

For more ideas, trails that are best for dogs in every state, and hiking tips, check out:

www.hikewithyourdog.com.

Bicycling

This outdoor exercise is good for you and good for your German Shepherd Dog if he is physically able and weather conditions permit. Bicycling with your dog requires a little bit of training for the outing to go well and for you to stay seated on your bike. Although you could simply grab your dog's leash and head out the door with your dog and your bike, for your safety—and the dog's—it's advisable to properly equip your bike and your dog.

For your dog, you will want to make sure he has a comfortable-fitting, non-restrictive harness—preferably one that is padded across the chest. It is also suggested to use a "bike" leash, which is quite a bit shorter than a six-foot every-day leash. There are specific leashes made for bike riding that attach to the bike's rear wheel. They are only a couple of feet long and stretch to absorb shock when your dog pulls out to the side. This specialized leash system allows your dog to trot closely to you and not dart in front of the bike. You will want to slowly acclimate him to trotting alongside your bike in an area that has as few distractions as possible. And, be careful in the beginning not to overexert your GSD. It is easy to do, as once you and your dog become acclimated to biking you will be able to cover more distance faster.

Be cognizant of the weather, heat, and temperature of the pavement and how it may affect your GSD. Cooler mornings are always preferable. Be cautious on warmer days when the pavement could heat up to pad-burning temperatures. In general, if you're not comfortable standing barefoot on the pavement for a solid minute without doing the hot lava dance, it's too hot for your dog to bike with you. Pack extra water for your dog and an emergency kit as described in "Camping/Hiking" on page 149.

Competitive Activities

Agility

Agility is, without doubt, the fastest growing dog sport in North America. The simple description of canine agility is that it is a sport in which the dog handler directs his or her dog through a predetermined course of jumps, tunnels, seesaws, and other obstacles in a race. It is judged both on time and a score based on how many errors the dog made in the course (knocked a pole down in a jump, missed a weave pole, almost missed an obstacle, etc.). The sport is always fresh and exciting for both handler and dog, as no two courses

have the same jumps and obstacles or the same order in which they are completed.

The sport of dog agility is easy to begin, as it is such a popular dog sport that many training clubs offer classes in agility, and there are also training clubs that focus only on agility. Agility is a great sport to keep a GSD mentally and physically active. It is also a great sport to help timid GSDs gain confidence, and can be a great way to bond with an adopted, adult GSD (if the dog doesn't have any structural issues, such as hip or elbow dysplasia). When looking for a training club to learn agility, search for a club in which the students are having a great time, where the emphasis is on having fun with your dog, and competition is only if you catch the agility "bug."

Barn Hunt

This sport is relatively new but is gaining popularity among dog owners. Barn Hunt is based on testing the traditional roles of many breeds that had to rid barns and farms of vermin. Any breed, whether originally trained for this work or not, can partake in barn hunts. The Barn Hunt Association (*www.barnhunt.com*) relates that any age dog (or handler) can have fun in this sport. The only stipulation for Barn Hunt trials is that the dog must fit through an 18-inch wide by bale-height tall tunnel, and that the competing dog has a Barn Hunt registration number. No registration number is required to take part in the Barn Hunt Fun Test.

The entire purpose of the Barn Hunt is to test the dog's ability to find tubes in a hay bale maze/course that has a live rat. Some tubes have nothing, some have rat litter (droppings), and one has a live rat.

To find a club that trains for Barn Hunt Trials, go to the sanctioning organization's website:

www.barnhunt.com.

Conformation

The great sport of dog showing is conformation. A dog may only compete in conformation if he or she is registered with the AKC and intact. Within the breed, male dogs are judged first, then females. Within each sex, there are a variety of classes, starting with six-month old puppies (the youngest a dog can be shown) and including "Open Dog"

class (any age dog but typically dogs more than a year old), Bred By Exhibitor, and American Bred. The winner of each class comes back into the ring to determine "Winners Dog." This dog receives a number of "points" toward his championship, depending on the number of the dogs he beat to be the top male dog that day. Then the same process takes place for the female dogs. Once a "Winners Bitch" has been awarded, the Winners Dog and Winners Bitch come back into the ring, along with all the dogs entered that have already achieved their championships. (To be awarded a championship, a dog must have earned 15 points with a minimum of two "major" wins—3 points or more—under two different judges.) The winner from all champions, Winners Dog, and Winners Bitch is awarded Best of Breed. The Best of Breed winner then goes on to compete in Group Competition. For the GSD, that is the Herding Group. Winners of each of the different breed groups then go on to compete for Best in Show.

The German Shepherd Dog's breed standard was originally based on the German GSD breed standard but has been modified and further developed by the German Shepherd Dog Club of America (GSDCA). This standard is used to determine how "correct" a dog is in looks, coat, teeth, and movement; however, dogs are judged against each other, so if a puppy class has

four spectacular puppies, only one will be selected to compete against the other winners of their respective classes. Professional handlers are present in almost all breeds; however, some well-respected breeders and owner-handlers have competed with their dogs and achieved championships. Whether you show yourself or hire a pro, the sport of dog showing is expensive. Dog show entries are not cheap and most owner handlers travel to many different states for dog shows virtually every weekend. Hotels, gas, meals on the road, etc., add up quickly, particularly if a dog is not winning.

Showing a GSD in United Kennel Club (UKC) dog shows is a bit different, as the club was founded to encourage the owner/breeder handler and prohibits the use of professional handlers in conformation classes. Dogs are judged against each other, as in the AKC dog show; however, each dog is rated by the judge against the breed standard and each individual is given a written rating and critique. Ratings are Excellent, Very Good, Acceptable, and Non-rated. UKC dog shows offer classes for intact dogs, as well as altered dogs.

Disc Dogs

The sport of disc dog competition began with a 19-year-old college student, a Whippet, and an idea that jumping the fence with his dog during a Major League Baseball game

(Los Angeles Dodgers vs. Cincinnati Reds) and tossing his dog a frisbee seemed like a good idea at the time. Turns out, security didn't really think so, but the nation and dog owning population thought it looked amazing. The year was 1974. The next year, Alex Stein (the Whippet-owning frisbee thrower), helped organize the Frisbee Dog World Championships. Stein and his dog, Ashley, won the first three years of competition. In 1980, the championships were renamed "Ashley Whippet Invitational," in honor of Ashley, and the competition continues to this day.

In addition to the annual invitational, SkyHoundz offers Disc Dog competitions throughout the United States and internationally.

SkyHoundz also offers training videos and a book, *Disc Dogs! The Complete Guide*, by Peter Bloeme and Jeff Perry, to help dog owners break into the sport of frisbee catching.

Within the disc dog community, there are several different classifications (Classic, DiscDogathon, and Xtreme Distance), as well as events scored on speed and accuracy and "freestyle."

German Shepherd Dogs that love to retrieve and that are physically fit (and with no hip or elbow disease) may be great candidates for this sport. The handler also needs to be able to throw a disc with strength and accuracy. To get involved or to find a training club, contact SkyHoundz at *www.skyhoundz.com*.

Dock Jumping

If your GSD loves to retrieve and enjoys water, how much fun would he have jumping off a state-of-the-art dock and competing for the fastest retrieve or the longest or highest jump into water? This sport does not involve much training and draws a lot of crowds. The competitions are sanctioned by the UKC and DockDogs (*www.dockdogs.com*). And, if you think this is a backyard type of sport, think again. The distance the dogs travel (either up or out) is measured with a digital video capture system using enhanced measurement system software. The system, which was developed for use in Olympic events, measures from the end of the dock to the point at which the dog's tail set enters the water.

With all the high-tech equipment used for the events, it is still designed as a sport to encourage the everyday owner and everyday dog to come out and have some family fun.

Flyball

If your GSD is crazy about balls—not just halfway interested but *crazy*—the sport of flyball might be fun to look into as a dog sport. To participate in flyball events, your GSD will need to be on a flyball team. Teams are made of four dogs. In competition, the team's time begins when the first dog crosses the start line. The course is straight, 51-feet long, and has several hurdles (set to 4″ lower than the shoulder

height of the team's shortest dog). At the turn-around point is a box with a lever. The dog must stop on the lever and catch the ball that pops out of the box. With ball in mouth, the dog turns around and runs back over the hurdles. As soon as he crosses the start line, the second dog in the team is released. This continues until all four dogs have finished the course.

Flyball is very fast, requires training, and was it mentioned that the dog must love balls? Local clubs with teams can be found at the North American Flyball Association's (NAFA) website: *www.flyball.org*.

Herding

Your German Shepherd Dog is a descendant of some of the finest, versatile herding dogs ever created in Germany. Up until 2010, GSDs were still used on at least

one farm to control large (up to 1,000 sheep) flocks. The Verein für Deutsche Schäferhunde (the founding club of the GSD in Germany) has awarded many GSDs the Herdengebrauchshund (HGH) or Herding Dog Title. In the United States, you can compete with your GSD in herding trials held by the AKC, the American Herding Breed Association (*www.ahba-herding.org*), and the Australian Shepherd Club of America (*www.asca.org*).

Most tests and trials are structured around herding dogs that either fetch (go into the field, round up the livestock, and bring them back to the handler) or drive (a dog that pushes sheep out of the clipping shed and into a field after they've been shorn). In AKC herding trials, these tasks are tested on the "A" course or the "B" course. Livestock used in the tests can be sheep, cat-

tle, and ducks for courses A and B. Farming chores are tested with the new Farm Dog Certified Test.

The GSD has a different style of herding, which is classified as "tending." Tending is a form of herding specific to German Shepherd Dogs, Belgian Shepherds, and Briards. GSDs were tasked with moving large herds of sheep from pasture to pasture, across open farmlands, down narrow roads, and with no fences to help keep the sheep in one area. The tending herder also protected the sheep from predators and constantly patrolled the borders set for the flock. After a day of grazing, the tending herder gathered up the sheep and brought the sheep back "home." In AKC herding trials, the GSD will be tested on sheep only and in an open field course with a narrow road up to 880 yards long— or Course C.

Many GSD owners with an interest in herding compete on A courses, which involve moving up to five sheep through an obstacle course. This is not because that is the course of choice; rather, it is because it is difficult to find a farm in close proximity (within an hour) that has the sheep and a skilled tending-style trainer. Finding a trial with a C course can also be difficult, as it requires more sheep and a much larger area. In 2016, only three German Shepherd Dogs received herding titles.

If you're interested in herding, or if you're interested in testing your GSD on the Farm Dog Certification (which requires that the dog help you complete typical farm chores and be non-reactive to livestock), it is recommended that you and your GSD have an excellent dog-handler relationship (as he will be required to respond to your commands at a distance while working with livestock), that he has been introduced to and is comfortable around livestock, and that he has reached a level of maturity in which he will not be easily intimidated by sheep—which will not be much smaller than he is as an adult. Check out the AKC's herding page (*www.akc.org/events/herding*) for more information and to help locate a training club near you.

Internationale Prüfungs-Ordnung (IPO)

Formerly known as Schutzhund, IPO is a sport designed to test dogs in three phases: tracking, obedience, and protection. The Verein für Deutsche Schäferhunde (SV) developed the first Schutzhund test, as it was concerned that with the industrialization of Germany, the herding dog (GSD) would be carelessly bred for use as police and military dogs and the breed would suffer from careless breeding, which in turn would produce GSDs with undesirable traits, such as mental instability.

The SV held its first Shutzhund test in Germany in 1901 to demonstrate the German Shepherd Dog breed's trainability, along with his courage, endurance, mental stability, scenting ability, and willingness to work. Today, the sport is referred to as IPO and requires that you begin with an athletic, high-drive GSD that is also confident, calm, and well socialized. It is not a sport for a timid dog or one with serious dominance issues. It is also *not* training for a personal "attack" dog. IPO is first and foremost a *sport*. The IPO-trained GSD must pass all three phases of the competition in one day: Phase 1 is Tracking, Phase 2 is Obedience, and Phase 3 is Protection. A dog does not continue in the competition if he has failed a phase.

In Phase 3, the dog is tested on his ability to find a "suspect" and to seamlessly transform from launching his body full speed at a "helper" (the guy with all the pads on) and grabbing the heavily padded helper's right arm, to immediately calming, releasing the pad, and showing sociable, friendly behaviors on the command of his handler/owner.

It is critical that if you are interested in training your GSD for IPO work, that you find a well-qualified trainer and are comfortable with the training techniques being used. The GSD is a very forgiving training partner, but has often been trained with a heavy hand in this sport, sometimes creating dogs that were responding more out of fear than out of courage. Fearful dogs have no part in the sport of Schutzhund, as they must be able to go from full attack, to completely sociable, accepting dogs on command.

Not all GSDs are suitable for this type of work, and if you push and train under the wrong trainer, you can ruin a nice dog.

Note: You can participate in the obedience and tracking phases of the IPO event individually; there is no requirement to participate in all three phases unless you are seeking an IPO1, 2, or 3 title. Tracking titles without obedience or protection are TR1, TR2, and TR3. The obedience title, "Begleithund" (BH), is a combined obedience and temperament test that is required of all dogs prior to advancing to testing for an IPO title. Obedience titles without tracking or protection are OB1, OB2, and OB3.

For more information on IPO and training GSDs for this event, contact the United Schutzhund Clubs of America (USCA), an organization that is solely for GSDs and the sport of IPO: *www.germanshepherddog. com*. For all-breed IPO competitions, go to: American Working Dog Federation (AWDF) at *www.awdf.net*.

Lure Coursing

A sport that was originally designed to test the hunting abilities of sighthounds in an open field with broken field running, lure coursing is becoming a fun activity for nearly every breed that enjoys chasing. Lure coursing does not use live or deceased animals; rather, a "lure" made of plastic bags is pulled in a constantly changing course with the use of a string and pulley system, which is controlled by the course master. The AKC and the UKC offer lure coursing events.

With the AKC and the UKC, any breed can take part in the Coursing Ability Test (CAT). This non-competitive coursing test runs each dog individually, and if the dog shows enthusiasm, interest in the lure, and

finishes the course, he has passed the CAT. If your GSD really enjoys the sport, you can enter him in the AKC's "Fast CAT" competition, in which he is ranked according to the speed in which he finishes the course, with the handicap given for his breed.

Coursing is a great sport for physically able GSDs that have a lot of herding instinct and prey drive. If, however, your GSD is one that has shown yellow-light behaviors around small animals, this sport would not be recommended, as it encourages and heightens a dog's prey drive. The sport is great for first-time dog sport people, as it doesn't require anything other than the handler releasing the dog and catching him at the end.

Nose Work

The UKC and the National Association of Canine Scent Work (NACSW) offer a scent detection sport that is designed to be a safe and fun activity that allows dogs to use their natural scenting abilities. Nosework is a good fit for a wide range of GSDs, from high-drive working dogs to family pets.

The first requirement for the UKC's nosework event is a "pass" in the pre-trial class. The club that is holding the event will hold pre-trial classes for the specific odors, up to five, that are being tested at the trial. If the dog has passed the Odor Recognition Test (ORT) from the NACSW, he does not need to retest with the UKC's pre-trial class.

With the NACSW, the ORT requires that the dog search 12 identical boxes with only one containing an odor. The search is "blind," in that the handler does not know which box contains the odor.

The UKC event tests dogs on individual odors with varying difficulty: novice, advanced, superior, master, and elite. The odors are also tested in four different areas or enclosures: container, interior, vehicle, and exterior. The title for the Novice level with the scent search in a container would be NC, Novice level in an "interior" would be NI, Advanced level in a vehicle would be AV, Superior level in an "exterior" would be SE, and so on.

For more information on nosework and to find an active club or a nosework trainer near you, contact the UKC (*www.ukcdogs.com/ nosework*) and/or the NACSW (*www. nacsw.net*).

Obedience

The sport of obedience in the United States dates to 1933, when the first obedience trial was held in Mt. Kisko, New York. Participants were recorded as being two Labrador Retrievers, three Poodles, two English Springer Spaniels, and not surprisingly, one German Shepherd Dog. In 1936, the AKC approved the first set of regulations for "Obedience Test Field Trials," which had the same classifications under which dogs and handlers compete today: Novice, Open, and Utility.

Unlike sports that test a dog's training along with his inherent traits, such as herding, obedience tests the partnership between handler and dog through a series of exercises that are completely trained. At the novice level, exercises include: heeling on leash, making a figure eight while heeling, heeling off leash, stand for examination, recall, long sit (one minute), and long down (three minutes). To receive the Companion Dog (CD) title, the dog must pass the novice level test three times. The dog must have his CD title before he proceeds to testing for the next level, Companion Dog Excellent (CDX).

The UKC also offers obedience trials with very similar exercises, making it possible to compete relatively seamlessly between AKC and UKC sponsored obedience trials. The beauty of obedience trials is that they are only as competitive as you make them. You and your GSD can compete for the highest score in your class and highest score in trial. Or, if you're not competitive, you can enter obedience trials to earn a title, in which your goal is to earn a passing score and a "leg" toward your dog's title.

To find out more about this sport, go to the AKC's website: *www.akc.org/events/obedience/getting-started* or the UKC's website: *www.ukcdogs.com/obedience.*

Rally-Style Obedience

Sometimes considered the fun and fast entry level for obedience trials, rally-style obedience allows the handler to talk to the dog the entire time they are going through the course. With rally-style obedience, the course is set up like a road rally, in which the dog and handler must go to each station in a prescribed order, complete a task, and then go to the next station.

At the entry level, the dog and handler will go through ten to 15 stations. Each station has a sign that tells the dog-handler team what to do. The entry level includes exercises such as change pace (slow down or speed up), *sit-stay*, turn 360 degrees, and drop into a *down.* All dogs begin with a perfect score of 100, and points are deducted as mistakes are made during the course. A qualifying score is 70, and three qualifying scores under two different judges are required to earn a title. For those with a competitive spirit, ribbons are awarded for first through fourth place.

Rally obedience titles are: Rally Novice (RN), Rally Advanced (RA), Rally Excellent (RE), and Rally Advanced Excellent (RAE).

Tracking

The sport of tracking is a noncompetitive event with titles offered from the AKC and the tracking portion IPO events. The GSD tracks using a combination of skills that include scenting the ground to determine the disturbance created by the footstep or path taken by a person(s) and air scenting to pick

up the direction in which a person moved.

Tracking is a good sport for GSDs that need a job. It requires the dog to focus, as well as have self-confidence. Since the dog works alone with his handler, a dog that is not sociable with other dogs can successfully train and compete in tracking events. Tracking titles from the AKC include: Tracking Dog (TD), Tracking Dog Excellent (TDX), and Variable Surface Tracker (VST). If an AKC-registered GSD achieves all three titles, he is awarded the AKC's Champion Tracker (CT) title.

The entry level tracking test requires the dog to follow a 440-yard track with an item left on the trail. The trail is laid by a person up to two hours before the test. It is a "blind" test, as you and the dog do not know where the track is but the judge who is watching you does. The track may have up to three to

five changes of direction. The dog wears a harness and the handler follows on a tracking line, a minimum of 10 feet behind the dog. The test finishes with the dog successfully navigating the trail and indicating the object (without picking it up or disturbing it) at the end of the trail. The dog only needs to pass the test once to attain the title.

The TDX is more complicated, involving a scent track with up to seven changes of direction that is a minimum of half a mile long and was laid up to five hours before the test is run. The track also has a second track that crosses the first track. And, it has three articles that the dog must alert the handler to but not pick up, as in the first test.

The VST is similar to the other tests except it is held on all hard, non-vegetative surfaces, such as sidewalks, gravel, metal staircases, etc.

Home-Schooling: How to Register for Events Without Papers

To compete in AKC events or earn AKC titles, your GSD must have an AKC number. Your dog can have one of three types of numbers.

An AKC registration number: If your dog was bred from two AKC-registered GSDs, you should have been given your puppy's "papers" by the breeder. If your papers did not require you to neuter or spay your GSD, your dog can compete in all performance events and conformation with the AKC. If your puppy is altered, or was required to be altered in order to receive your pup's papers, he can compete in all events except conformation. The registration number that you received will be what you use to enter your dog in events. This number can also be used with a variety of other organizations that sanction performance dog events.

A PAL number (Purebred Alternative Listing): This registration number is given to dogs that do not have an AKC registration number but that are obviously purebred dogs. A PAL number will allow a GSD without registration papers (such as a GSD from a rescue or shelter) to compete in all events except conformation. In order to receive a PAL number, go to the following website and download the application: *www.akc.org/register/purebred-alternative-listing*.

In addition to the application, you will be required to submit a small fee, along with two recent and full color photographs of your dog. One image must be a full front view that shows the facial characteristics of the dog; the other image is to show the full side profile of the dog in a stand on a hard, flat surface (not grass).

An AKC Canine Partners number: If your German Shepherd Dog is mostly GSD and a little something else, he, too, can compete in a variety of sports, such as agility, obedience, rally, tracking, and coursing ability. Mixed breed dogs and dogs of unknown heritage that don't quite look 100 percent German Shepherd Dogs can enroll in the AKC Canine Partners program. To enroll your GSD mix in this program, go to the online enrollment form here: *www.akc.org/dog-owners/canine-partners*.

UKC Events

If your puppy has his UKC Permanent Registration certificate, you are good to compete in UKC events. Puppies can only receive a UKC Permanent Registration if the puppy's parents were both registered with the UKC and the breeder provided the puppy's UKC registration papers to you at the time of sale (or shortly thereafter).

If you don't have a UKC Permanent Registration certificate, you can apply for either a UKC Single Registration or a UKC Performance

Listing. The UKC Single Registration is a method for purebred GSDs registered with the AKC, the Canadian Kennel Club, the Kennel Club (Great Britain), or any FCI-affiliated registry to become registered with the UKC. You will need to complete an application and provide a copy of your dog's complete, three-generation pedigree, as well as three high-quality color photographs: a photo of the dog standing from each side and one from the front. A small registration fee is required, too.

UKC Performance Listing (PL): If your GSD is a purebred dog of unknown pedigree (a rescued GSD, for example), a GSD with a little something else in him, or a purebred dog but with UKC breed standard disqualifications, you can apply for a PL through the UKC at the website: *www.ukcdogs.com/performance-listing*.

Useful Addresses and Literature

All-Breed Registries
American Kennel Club
8051 Arco Corporate Drive,
    Suite 100
Raleigh, NC 27617
919-233-9767
www.akc.org; info@akc.org

United Kennel Club
100 E. Kilgore Road
Kalamazoo, MI 49002
262-343-9020
www.ukcdogs.com

Breed Clubs
**German Shepherd Dog Club
    of America**
775-392-2913
www.gsdca.org; office@gsdca.org

**German Shepherd Dog Club
    of America—Working Dogs
    Association**
P.O. Box 5021
Woodland Hills, CA 91365
747-900-6805
www.gsdca-wda.org; GSDCA.
    WDA@gmail.com

**Verein für Deutsche
    Schäferhunde (SV) e.V.**
Steinerne Furt 71
86167 Augsburg
Germany
Phone: +49 0821 74002-0
www.schaeferhunde.de; info@
    schaeferhunde.de

Activities/Performance Events
American Kennel Club (AKC)
See listing under "All-Breed
    Registries"

**Canine Performance Events, Inc.
    (CPE)**
P.O. Box 805
South Lyon, MI 48178
www.k9cpe.com; cpe@charter.net

Animal-Assisted Therapy
Pet Partners
875 124th Avenue, NE, Suite 101
Bellevue, WA 98005
www.petpartners.org

Therapy Dog International, Inc.
88 Bartley Road
Flanders, NJ 07836
973-252-9800
www.tdi-dog.org

Therapy Dogs United (TDU)
1932B West 8th Street
Erie, PA 16505
www.therapydogsunited.org

**R.E.A.D. (Reading Education
    Assistance Program)**
Intermountain Therapy Animals
P.O. Box 17201
Salt Lake City, UT 84117
801-272-4339
www.therapyanimals.org/read;
    info@therapyanimals.org

AKC STAR Program
See "American Kennel Club" listing

Barn Hunt
Barn Hunt Association (BHA)
www.barnhunt.com

Canine Good Citizen
See "American Kennel Club" listing

Conformation
See "American Kennel Club" listing
See "United Kennel Club" listing

Disc Dog
Ashley Whippet Invitational (AWI)
www.ashleywhippet.com

SkyHoundz
660 Hembree Parkway, Suite 110
Roswell, GA 30076
770-751-3882
www.skyhoundz.com;
    customerservice@skyhoundz.com

Dock Jumping
DockDogs
5183 Silver Maple Lane
Medina, OH 44256
330-241-4975
www.dockdogs.com; info@
    dockdogs.com

See "United Kennel Club" listing

Flyball
North American Flyball Association
    (NAFA)
1333 West Devon Avenue, #512
Chicago, IL 60660
www.flyball.org

Herding
**American Herding Breed
    Association (AHBA)**
www.ahba-herding.org

See "American Kennel Club" listing

**Australian Shepherd Club of
    America (ASCA)**
ASCA Business Office
6091 E. State Hwy 21
Bryan, TX 77808
979-778-1082
www.asca.org

IPO/Schutzhund
American Working Dog Foundation
www.awdf.net

See "German Shepherd Dog Club
of America—Working Dogs
Association" listing

**United Schutzhund Clubs of
America**
4407 Meramec Bottom Road,
Suite J
St. Louis, MO 63129
314-638-9686
www.germanshepherddog.com

Nose Work
**National Association of Canine
Scent Work (NACSW)**
www.nacsw.net

See "United Kennel Club" listing

Obedience
See "American Kennel Club" listing
See "United Kennel Club" listing

Rally-Style Obedience
See "American Kennel Club" listing
See "United Kennel Club" listing

World Cynosport Rally
P.O. Box 850955
Richardston, TX 75085-0955
www.rallydogs.com

Resources

Aloff, Brenda. *Aggression in Dogs:
Practical Management, Prevention
& Behaviour Modification.* Direct
Book Service, 2004.
Abrantes, Roger. *Dog Language: An
Encyclopedia of Canine Behavior.*
Direct Book Service, 1997.
Bulanda, Susan. *Ready! Training
of the Search and Rescue Dog.*
Lumina Media, 2014.
Burch, Mary R., PhD, and Jon S.
Bailey, PhD. *How Dogs Learn.*
Howell Book House, 1999.
McConnell, Patricia B., PhD. *The
Other End of the Leash.* Reprint.
Ballentine Books, 2003.
Miller, Pat, CPDT, CDBC. *Positive
Perspectives 2: Know Your Dog,
Train Your Dog.* Dogwise, 2008.
Wilde, Nicole, CPDT. *Getting a GRIP
on Aggression Cases: Practical
Consideration for Dog Trainers.*
Phantom Publishers, 2008.

Index

Activities
  competitive, 151–161
  non-competitive events/
    programs, 143–146
  non-competitive service,
    146–149
  outdoor, 149–151
Activity level, high, 19–20
Aggression, 127–128.
    See also dog-on-dog
    aggression
  babies/children, 135–136
  barrier, 136–137
  chase/predatory, 133–134
  fear, 129, 132–133
  food-related, 137–138
  from medications, 140
  frustration-elicited, 136–137
  health-related, 140
  hyperactive, 141
  maternal, 140
  medically based, 139
  owner-directed, 128–129
  pain, 140
  play, 138–139
  possessive, 134–135
  preventive measures, 128,
    130–139, 141
  reactive, 141
  redirected, 136–137
  seizure-related, 140
  sex-related, 141
  signs of, 129, 130
  social, 139
  territorial/protective,
    129–131
Agility, 20, 151, 162
AKC Canine Partners, 162
AKC registration number, 162
AKC S.T.A.R. Puppy
    Program, 143

Anxiety, travel, 80–81
Anxious, 52, 54–56, 60, 75

Barking/whining, 117–118
Barn hunt, 152
Bedtime, 42–44
Behaviors, 49–51
  displacement, 54
  green-light, 51–52
  making yellow-light green,
    55–56
  problem intervention, 5
  red-light, 54–55
  yellow-light, 52–54
Bicycling, 150–151
Body language, 48–49
Bolting, 118–119
Book resources, 167
Breakfast, 41

Camping/hiking, 149–150
Canine Good Citizen (CGC),
    143–144
Car harnesses, 79
Car sickness, 81
Car travel, 79–82
Characteristics and drives,
    17–24
Chewing, destructive, 122
Children, 4, 16–18, 25,
    32–33, 58
  rules for, 59
  rules for parents with, 58
Collar, 85–86
Commands
  collar touch, 97–98
  come, 104–106
  down, 102–103
  heel, 106–107
  here or *watch me*, 95–97
  leave it, 113

off and *up*, 109–111
sit, 99–100
stand, 111–112
stay, 100–102
take it and *out*, 112–113
Community Canine (Canine
    Good Citizen Advanced
    (CGCA)), 144–145
Conditioning for car travel,
    81–82
Conformation (dog
    showing), 152–153
Counter surfing, 120–121
Courage, 23–24
Crate, 38–41, 70, 72

Desensitization methods, 76
Digging, 122–123
Dinner, 42
Disc dogs, 153–154
Dock jumping, 155
Doggie daycares, 64
Dog-on-dog aggression.
    See also aggression
  dominance, 131
  fear, 132–133
  pack (siblings), 131–132
Dog's advocate, 49

Emotional support dog, 17
Event registering without
    papers, 162–163
Exercise, 74–75, 80, 90, 92
  importance of, 115–116

Fence jumping, 123–124
Flyball, 155
Focus intensity, 21–22

Genetics versus
    environment, 47–48

German Shepherd
history of, 7–16
untrained dog, 1–3
well-trained dog, 3–5
Get back, teaching, 120
"Go potty!" command, 42
"Gotta go" cues, 37–41

Herding, 8, 17–18, 155–157
Home habituation, 69–70
for rescued dogs, 82–83
Hormonal drives, 24
Housetraining, 35–45

"I'll be back" training, 74–76
Independent thinking, 22
Internationale Prüfungs-
Ordnung (IPO), 157–158

Jumping up, 124–125

Learning capabilities by age,
27–31
Leash, 86
Light chasing, 78–79
Literature and addresses,
165–166
Lure coursing, 158–159
Lures: what to use, 86

Mental stimulation, 3–4,
115–116, 118, 123, 125,
141
Military dog, 12–13, 17
Mouthing, 2, 116–117

Noise aversion, 77–78
Nosework, 159

Obedience, 159–160

PAL number, 162
Pee pads, 43
Play groups, 64–65
Play/training session, 41
Police K-9s, 13–14, 17
Prey/play drive, high, 19
Prick ear shape, 7
Protective instincts, 18–19
Punish, don't, 69

Puppy
dog-friendly/nondog
places, 57–58
"food in/poop out"
schedule, 41
"gotta go" cues, 37–38
not vaccinated, 59–60
urges and abilities, 35–37
vaccinated dog, 60–62,
64–65
vaccinations, 57
vaccinations not complete,
63–64
where not to take puppy,
63

Quiet, teaching, 118

Rally-style obedience, 160
Reinforcement
negative, 24, 116
positive, 4, 27, 56, 70, 88,
90
Rescued dog, 32–33, 44–45
socialization of, 65–67
Rescued dogs
home habituation for, 82–83
Rest/naptime, 42
Routine, creating, 41–44
Rules for children, 59
Rules for parents with
children, 58

Search and rescue (SAR),
13, 146–147
Self-mutilation, 125
Sense of smell, 22–23
Separation anxiety (SA)
preventing, 72–76
treating, 73–74
Service dogs, 14–15
Shopping carts, 57–58
Sights and sounds, 69–70
Socialization
with dogs, 62–65
with people, 56–59
of rescued dog, 65–67
Spay/neuter, 24
Strength, 23
Swimming, 149

Therapy Dogs, 16–17,
147–149
Thunderstorms, 76–77
Tracking, 160–161
Trainer/training school
benefits of, 91
finding good, 91–92
Training. *See also*
reinforcement
challenges, 24–25
clicker training basics,
93
daily training routine, 3
learning a new behavior,
86–88
learning by association, 87
no hesitation rule, 60
no repeat rule, 90–91
place, 70–71
stop on a good note, 97
timing, 89–91
tools, 85–86
voice command and final
action, 87–88
Trash can bandits, 121
Travel, 4–5
Travel anxiety, 80–81
Treats, 50, 60–62, 66, 70,
80, 82, 85
Types of German
Shepherds
backyard dogs, 21
show lines, 20
working/performance
lines, 20

UKC Events, 162–163
UKC Performance Listing
(PL), 163
Unattended dog, 80
Urban Canine Good Citizen
(CGCU), 146

Veterinarian, 40, 45, 60, 63,
76, 78, 80–82, 92

Wait, teaching, 119–120
Wakeup, 41
War dog, 8–11
Watchdog abilities, 18